Healthy

Living

Cookbook

rosemary stanton
healthy living cookbook

MACMILLAN
Pan Macmillan Australia

For Peter
and our children,
Matthew, Katrina, Annabel and Meaghan,
who were all good eaters as children,
and have now turned out to be good cooks.

First published 1998 in Macmillan by Pan Macmillan Australia Pty Limited
St Martins Tower, 31 Market Street, Sydney
Reprinted 1999
Copyright © Rosemary Stanton 1998

National Library of Australia
cataloguing-in-publication data:

Stanton, Rosemary
Healthy living cookbook.

ISBN 0 7329 0923 6

1. Cookery (Natural foods). I. Title.

641.563

Designed by Guy Mirabella and Rob Cowpe
Printed in Hong Kong by Toppan Printing

Contents

Preface   vii

Introduction   ix

Breakfasts   1

Soups   14

Pasta, Rice and Grains   27

Seafood   49

Poultry and Meats   67

Legumes   96

Vegetables   112

Salads   138

Sauces and Dressings   156

Desserts   171

Muffin, Loaves and Sweet Treats   186

Index   200

Preface

Some people have the idea that if it tastes good it must be bad for you. Nothing could be further from the truth.

I absolutely love sitting down to a good meal and I don't want to waste any meal of my life eating something that does not taste great. I especially don't want to insult my tastebuds – or my body – by eating junk. Food should be positively enjoyable, nourishing the body, soul and senses.

For many people, a real love of good food has been superseded by a pattern of eating that is as easy and convenient as possible – preferably not involving much time or thought. That is sad because cooking is fun and taking time to sit down and enjoy a really good meal with family or friends is one of life's great pleasures.

Many people complain they don't have time to cook. Having had four children and a demanding career that runs on tight deadlines, I have a great understanding of time pressures. We can't fit in everything. But try to devote some time to cooking because the alternative of eating packaged or take-away foods is a nutritionist's nightmare and provides little delight to the tastebuds. Fast foods and ready-to-eat items are designed to be convenient and to have no flavour to which anyone objects. What a pathetic loss of potential enjoyment!

An American nutritionist and environmentalist studied the time people spend on food, in shopping, planning, cooking and eating and found that people take more time shopping now than they did 50 years ago but use less time planning, cooking and eating meals.

The increased time shopping is largely because of the enormous number of food items you have to work through to find what you really want. Before the 1960s we had 600-800 foods available. We now have 15,000 – some of them new and wonderful varieties of fruits and vegetables, but most variations on a theme of artificially flavoured and coloured junk.

The decrease in planning, cooking and eating time has been largely taken up by increased time spent watching television. Over 50 per cent of Australian families now share their fast evening meal with a television set rather than with each other.

I have always found that cooking was the best part of my daily chores, although I admit I love a day off sometimes. Most women don't actually mind cooking, they dislike having to take responsibility for planning meals and having to cook seven days a week. But cooking sure beats ironing or cleaning the bathroom and is infinitely more satisfying than tidying children's bedrooms.

Women need to teach men and children how to cook so they can take a turn. That way, it isn't a chore for anyone. Start young. A three-year-old can tear up leaves for a salad. All children love to make bread and the feeling of cleverness you – or they – get when a wonderfully fragrant hot loaf emerges from the oven is one of life's simple pleasures, overtaken only by the delight of eating it. This is applause cooking at its finest. And men and children need applause for their efforts. Let's give it to them, for only if cooking and food preparation tasks are shared among family members will we have any hope of stemming the tide of fast foods that is threatening to engulf us – ruining our tastebuds and health in one clean sweep.

It's not too late. So let's make at least one meal every day a time when the family can enjoy good food, talk, laugh – even argue – but get together to share something worthwhile.

I hope these recipes help all family members to enjoy cooking and discover that healthy food can taste good.

Introduction

HEALTHY EATING

Nutrition is a constantly changing science. Every day there are new findings as foods slowly yield their secrets.

We thought we knew a lot about nutrition a few years ago, and most nutritionists considered that foods were a collection of proteins, fats, carbohydrate, fibre, minerals and vitamins. We now know that foods contain several thousand components and many have values we previously ignored or wrongly attributed to vitamins.

Apart from breast milk, which supplies all nutritional needs for the first six months of life, no one food has everything. But the most wonderful foods in the diet – and the most neglected – are plant foods. They are particularly rich in compounds that decrease the risk of problems such as heart disease and various cancers. We all need to eat more plant-based foods, choosing as wide a variety as possible to ensure the best intake of nutrients.

Although a diet based solely on plant foods can meet most of our nutritional needs, the task of feeding the body well is much easier if we include some other foods. Seafoods are especially valuable. Dairy products are also excellent sources of calcium – the nutrient most likely to be in short supply in many diets. If you choose to eat poultry and meat, you will also have a good source of iron, protein, zinc and many other minerals and vitamins. As long as meat does not dominate the diet and displace plant foods, there is no harm in eating it a couple of times a week.

The typical Western diet should have improved over the past few years as a wider variety of fruits, vegetables, seafoods and grain products has become available. Unfortunately, this has not happened and the diet is getting worse, mainly because people eat so many fast foods and ready-packaged, processed meals. With very few exceptions, these foods are high in fat, salt and sugar and most lack sufficient dietary fibre.

As a result of dietary choices, health problems are common. In countries such as Australia, the population is growing steadily fatter, gaining on average 1 gram of fat per day.

The incidence of coronary heart disease has almost halved since the late 1960s but is still much higher than in Mediterranean countries or Japan. Out of a population of 18 million people, 2.5 million take medication for high blood pressure. Bowel and breast cancers are among the highest levels in the world, gallstones are common and adult-onset diabetes is increasing at an alarming rate. Even dental decay, a disease that many people thought had disappeared since fluoride entered the water supply and toothpaste, is still common and is the most expensive of all the diet-related health problems.

Although many people overeat, a lot of women deliberately undereat, starving their bodies of nutrients by rejecting meals. Often they then break out and eat a heap of junk food, immediately feel guilty and go back to semi-starvation. This is a crazy and unhealthy way to eat. It is a modern phenomenon, related to the desire of many women to be extremely thin.

There are also many diet and health fads which can lead to a poor quality diet. Some people then try to compensate for this with pills, but nothing can take the place of good food.

Some of the crazy and confusing ideas about food and diet often come from people who are not qualified nutritionists. Some people become obsessed with single ideas about some particular food and fail to look at the diet as a whole. We certainly are what we eat, and it is important to look carefully at the total diet.

In a healthy diet, nothing needs to be omitted, but some foods should be given a greater role than others. Those that make a good contribution take the centre stage while less nutritious items should show up only occasionally.

The rules of healthy eating are as follows:

- **Eat most** of fruits, vegetables, breads, cereals and grains.
- **Eat moderately** of chicken, lean meat, eggs and dairy products, or choose vegetarian alternatives. Seafoods should have a place in the diet if possible.
- **Eat least** of saturated fats, sugar and salt.

Most common health problems go hand in hand with inactivity. Many people drive everywhere, have sedentary jobs and are in too much of a rush to be physically active. Without enough activity, the body's appetite control mechanism does not work properly and so many people overeat. Physical activity needs a diet rich in carbohydrate with enough minerals, vitamins, proteins and essential fatty acids to enable muscles to function properly.

FATS

It is not fats themselves that are a major problem – although all fats are potentially fattening – but saturated fats. These were once found mainly in meat and dairy products and some people thought all they needed to do was avoid animal fats. These days, much of our saturated fat comes from saturated vegetable fats. Coconut and palm kernel oil are used in many processed foods. Both are more highly saturated than beef dripping or lard.

Some fats processed from vegetable oils also end up high in either saturated or trans fatty acids as a result of the processing. Both these types of fat are undesirable, and some medical researchers believe that trans fatty acids produced in margarines and commercial-use vegetable fats are the worst type of all. The presence of these fatty acids is not declared on labels and they masquerade as monounsaturated fats, making it difficult for consumers.

Naturally-occurring monounsaturated fats in olive, macadamia or canola oil are quite safe and chemically different from the trans fatty acids found in processed fats. Unfortunately, canola oil used in many commercial fried and processed foods has the highest level of trans fatty acids of any fat. In the home, you are best sticking with time-honoured olive oil, or use macadamia oil.

Polyunsaturated fats come in two types: the omega 6 variety found in vegetable oils and margarines and omega 3 fats found in linseeds, canola oil, green vegetables and especially in fish and other seafood. The two types of polyunsaturated fats need to be balanced. Most people in Western countries who use polyunsaturated margarines have a gross imbalance and need to give up margarine and eat more fish. For those who cannot do without a spread a monounsaturated margarine, without trans fatty acids, is the best of a bad lot. Butter tastes good but has too much saturated fat to be used in any quantity.

Most people say they are using less fat and few admit to liking fat, so surveys report a decreasing fat intake. However, we are eating more fat but we just don't realise it. Sales of high-fat items continue to grow. Most people now buy lean meat but the fat that is trimmed off meat is either added to sausages and mince or sold back to food manufacturers to turn up in French fries from fast food outlets, pastries, biscuits and even frozen waffles!

Australians now spend one third of their food dollar on fast foods and take-away items. (The figure is even higher in the United States.) These foods are fatty, often with higher fat levels than in the past. For example, an old-fashioned hamburger averaged 18 grams of fat. The modern-day, fast food burger ranges from 27 to 35 grams. Most people are surprised at these figures as the fast food offerings coming from their clean surroundings don't seem fatty. The high levels of fat come from the high-fat, squishy, dissolving bun, the meat, cheese and sauce. Add a serve of small French fries (thin ones soak up more fat than larger fries) and you have more than enough fat for the entire day. We now eat more fat than any previous generation – much of it hidden in the processed and fast foods which dominate many people's diets.

A high-fat diet easily contributes to excess weight as fats have more than twice as many kilojoules as either proteins or carbohydrates. Too much saturated fat is also involved in coronary heart disease, high blood pressure, non-insulin-dependent diabetes, gallstones and certain types of cancer.

We do not need to avoid all fats. Some fats are essential. The best ones come from olive oil, nuts, avocado, macadamia oil and fish. In these foods, fats come with protective antioxidants that prevent fats doing any damage. With a product such as olive oil, this protection comes not only inside the body but also in the frypan. Unlike polyunsaturated fats which should never be re-used because their fats break down to undesirable compounds, olive oil can safely be re-used many times.

For those needing to lose weight, it makes sense to restrict all fats. Try to:

- use less cooking fat
- always heat your pan or wok and then add a little olive oil
- grill, barbecue, make casseroles without added fats, use the microwave or wrap foods in foil before baking
- look for fast foods with less fat, such as grilled fish or any other seafood, chargrilled skinless chicken, sandwiches, rolls, salads, fruit salads and low-fat yoghurt, hamburgers made with plenty of salad and lean meat
- choose lean cuts of meat and avoid foods in which 'beef fat' is listed as a major ingredient
- choose low-fat milks and yoghurt, less cheese and keep ice-cream as a special occasion food
- remove skin from poultry
- eat more low-fat foods such as fruits and vegetables, breads, grains and cereal foods, legumes, fish or lean chicken, and less cakes, biscuits, pastries and rich desserts.

SUGAR

There is probably nothing wrong with eating some sweet foods occasionally. The major points against refined sugar are that it:

- has no essential nutrients – no protein, no essential fats, no minerals, vitamins or dietary fibre
- makes fats taste nice (you wouldn't eat chocolate, biscuits, cakes, pastries, ice-cream or many desserts if the sugar didn't make the fat taste better)
- can easily replace other more nutritious foods in the diet (for example, grabbing a sweet bar for lunch instead of taking the time to get a sandwich and some fresh fruit)
- is so ubiquitous in foods that the average Australian gets through 230 teaspoons a week!

There is no need to be fanatical about cutting out all sugar but large amounts from foods such as soft drinks, highly sweetened breakfast cereals, and confectionery are best avoided. Sugar eaten at times when teeth cannot be brushed contributes to dental decay.

SALT

Once tastebuds get used to eating salty foods it becomes a habit. Like most habits, the taste for salt can be broken – given time. Most people's tastebuds take several months to become used to eating foods with less salt. Try gradually to cut back on salt and replace it with foods subtly seasoned with lemon or lime, herbs, spices or wine.

Salt adds flavour to foods but this is mainly the flavour of salt! Once your tastebuds become accustomed to less salt, they begin to pick up the natural flavours of other foods. Most people who stop adding salt and eating salty foods report that their food tastes better than ever before.

A high-salt diet contributes to high blood pressure in some people. As we have no way of knowing if we are to fall victim to this common condition, it makes sense for everyone to eat less salt.

We all need the components of salt – sodium and chloride – but there is little danger of anyone not getting enough as they are found naturally in many foods.

DIETARY FIBRE AND STARCH

Fibre and starch occur in all breads and cereals (fibre is especially high in wholemeal and wholegrain breads and cereal products); grains and grain products such as pasta, polenta, cracked wheat, couscous and rice; legumes; nuts and seeds; and potatoes. Fruits are good sources of dietary fibre. With the exception of nuts, all high-fibre foods have little or no fat. With nuts, at least the fats are a healthy type and come in association with a wide range of highly protective substances.

Contrary to popular belief, starchy foods are not fattening. The body can convert carbohydrate to fat but only does so when the quantity is huge – equal to the amount of carbohydrate in more than 30 slices of bread. Carbohydrate is not stored so you can't accumulate a small excess. In fact, almost no-one can eat enough carbohydrate for it to be converted to fat. Instead carbohydrate stimulates the metabolism and any excess refills the muscles ready for exercise or is burned as fuel.

If you are trying to lose weight, you may need to put some restriction on carbohydrate or it will supply the body with all the energy it needs and it won't get round to using its supply of stored energy from fat.

The many so-called slimming diets that tell you to avoid foods which are rich in carbohydrates 'work' because they lead to a temporary loss of the body's normal water as well as some more damaging and permanent loss of lean muscle tissue. Avoid such diets.

Carbohydrates are good, filling foods and this book includes some easy and interesting recipes for high-carbohydrate foods. There is also a chapter on legumes (dried beans and peas) as they are among the most useful of foods. Many people don't eat them because they are not sure how to prepare them.

VITAMINS AND MINERALS

If your diet is lacking in vitamins, you should try to change the diet. Adding pills to a poor diet does not make up for what is missing.

Sometimes minerals such as calcium or iron are helpful when there is a known deficiency. Never take extra iron unless you know from blood tests that your iron levels are low. Excess iron is undesirable and can interfere with the absorption of other minerals such as zinc and copper.

There is no truth to claims made by those selling vitamins that modern foods lack vitamins. Plants store vitamins for their own sake and if they don't have enough of any nutrient, they don't grow properly.

Organic produce is best because it helps protect the fragile environment of the earth, but whether organically grown or not, produce is an excellent source of nutrients. Only some forms of processing destroy the natural goodness of foods.

Adding vitamins to a poorly chosen diet does not fix the problems caused by excess fat, sugar, salt and alcohol and a lack of complex carbohydrate and dietary fibre. Adding vitamins simply gives a false sense of security. The Australian food supply is rich in essential nutrients. All you need to do is to make the right choices. Simply follow the principles mentioned earlier and your diet can supply all your needs.

PROTEIN

Some people are concerned that they may not be getting enough protein. For most people, such concerns are unnecessary – most Australians eat far more protein than the body needs.

ANTIOXIDANTS AND OTHER PROTECTIVE FACTORS

A wide range of several thousand of these compounds occur in foods. Rich sources are fruits and vegetables, legumes, nuts, seeds, olive oil, red wine and wholegrain products.

Many are well preserved in cooked foods but a few are lost. Try to include a variety of both cooked and raw items in your daily diet.

SUMMARY

Healthy eating is neither difficult nor expensive. Ready-prepared foods are far more likely to strain the household budget and if you choose these items poorly, you don't even get nutritional value for your money.

All the healthy food in the world won't do you an ounce of good if it doesn't taste good too. Healthy eating and good cooking go hand in hand.

The recipes in this book have been designed for those who don't have a lot of time to spend in the kitchen. They are the kind of foods which my family eat regularly. And, perhaps most important of all, they taste good.

breakfasts

Breakfast is the most important meal of the day. It really gets the body going after the overnight fast. An ideal breakfast includes some fresh fruit, cereal (either a hot porridge or a nutritious cold cereal) and some wholemeal toast with a little marmalade, jam, honey or Vegemite. If you like a cooked breakfast, add a boiled or poached egg, mushrooms, corn or baked beans on toast.

If you really cannot face breakfast first thing in the morning, try to have a nutritious snack by 9 or 10 o'clock. Yoghurt with fruit, a slice of wholemeal bread wrapped round a banana, some toast, a wholemeal roll, a sandwich or some whole rye or wheat crispbread would be suitable.

WINTER FRUIT SALAD

1 Combine fruits, juice, cinnamon stick, honey and rind. Bring to the boil, cover and leave overnight.

An ideal breakfast for chilly winter mornings when you still want something light.

2 Remove cinnamon stick. Serve fruits topped with yoghurt and almonds.

Nutritional information/serving: 3.5 g fat, 4.5 g fibre, 920 kJ.

Serves 4		
½ cup dried apples	Piece cinnamon stick	
½ cup dried peaches or nectarines	1 teaspoon honey	
½ cup prunes	1 teaspoon finely grated orange rind (no pith)	
¼ cup raisins	200 g carton natural yoghurt	
1 cup apple juice	1 tablespoon toasted flaked almonds	

Handy Hint
A short walk or an early morning swim improves your appetite for breakfast.

TOASTED MUESLI

1 Preheat oven to 180°C. Spread oats on an ungreased oven tray and bake for about 10-15 minutes, stirring several times until oats are golden brown (take care they don't burn). Allow to cool.

2 Toast sesame, coconut and almonds by the same method. Cool.

3 Mix in remaining ingredients.

Most commercial toasted mueslis are made by soaking the ingredients in saturated vegetable fat and sugar and baking the mixture. This recipe has no added fat or sugar and is delicious.

Nutritional information/serving: 7 g fat, 5 g fibre, 870 kJ.

Makes 30-50 serves

750 g rolled oats
¼ cup sesame seeds
1 cup coconut flakes
½ cup flaked almonds
250 g rye or barley flakes (available from health food shops)
1 cup wheatgerm

300 g dried fruit medley (pieces of apricot, apple, peach and sultanas)
250 g sultanas
½ cup pepitas
1 cup sunflower seeds
½ cup roasted buckwheat

SWISS MUESLI

1 Combine oats, milk and honey and leave soaking in the refrigerator overnight. Next morning, add apples, hazelnuts and yoghurt.

True Swiss muesli is not a dry cereal. It is partly prepared the night before, so that the oats have softened by morning.

Nutritional information/serving: 10 g fat, 6 g fibre, 1440 kJ.

Serves 4	2 cups rolled oats	2 apples, cored and grated
	1 cup fat-reduced milk	¼ cup chopped hazelnuts
	1 tablespoon honey	1 cup low-fat yoghurt

Handy Hint
Never skip breakfast. The body reduces its metabolic rate and burns fewer kilojoules during the entire day if you skip breakfast.

OAT BRAN CREPES

1 Place all ingredients in blender, mix well. Stand for up to 1 hour, or refrigerate overnight.

This can be either a dessert or a breakfast dish.

2 Heat frypan and brush with light olive oil. Pour crepe mixture into pan (if too thick to pour, add a little more milk). Cook over moderate heat until golden brown, flip over and brown other side.

Serve with lemon juice or berries or stewed or canned fruit (no added sugar).

Nutritional information/serving: 2 g fat, 2 g fibre, 270 kJ.

Makes 12 small crepes, serves 6	cup oat bran	¾ teaspoon bi-carbonate of soda
	1½ cups buttermilk	2 teaspoons sugar (optional)
	1 egg	Extra milk, if required
	½ cup wholemeal plain flour	

OATCAKES

1 Warm milk to lukewarm, add honey and yeast and leave to stand for 5 minutes.

A good dish for brunch.

2 Add oat bran and oats, mix well and stand for 30 minutes.

3 Heat a large non-stick frypan and brush with a little light olive oil. Pour about 2 tablespoons of mixture into pan, cook until brown on one side then turn and cook other side. Repeat with remaining mixture.

Serve warm with honey or fruit spread.

Nutritional information/serving: 3 g fat, 2.5 g fibre, 505 kJ.

Makes 6
2 cups low-fat milk
1 teaspoon honey
7 g packet of yeast
¼ cup oat bran
1 cup 1-minute oats

OATY VEGETABLE OMELETTE

1 Heat a non-stick pan and brush with olive oil. Add mushrooms and tomato and cook over a gentle heat for 3-4 minutes. Add parsley and oats and stir to combine.

A new way to combine oats and a cooked breakfast.

2 Beat eggs with water and pour over mushroom mixture in pan. Cook over a gentle heat, gently lifting egg mixture to allow any uncooked mixture to run underneath, until set. Sprinkle with pepper.

Nutritional information/serving: 9 g fat, 3 g fibre, 750 kJ.

Serves 2

1 cup sliced mushrooms
1 medium tomato, sliced
1 tablespoon chopped parsley
⅓ cup rolled oats

3 eggs
1 tablespoon water
Freshly ground pepper

FRENCH TOAST

1 Beat together milk, cinnamon, rind and egg. Dip bread into mixture, allowing it to soak in.

2 Heat a non-stick frypan, brush with a little melted butter and cook toast until brown on both sides. Sprinkle with sugar and serve immediately.

Nutritional information/serving: 7.5 g fat, 2 g fibre, 1155 kJ.

Makes 2 slices, serves 1

For each person:
½ cup skim milk
Pinch cinnamon
1 teaspoon finely chopped lemon rind

1 egg
2 slices spicy fruit loaf
1 teaspoon sugar

MARMALADE IN THE MICROWAVE

1 Slice all fruits finely. Cover with water and microwave on high for 20 minutes or until peel is very soft.

If you have never made marmalade, this recipe is an ideal starting point. Using the microwave means you do not have burnt jam. Citrus peel is an excellent source of pectin, a valuable form of soluble dietary fibre.

2 Measure quantity of fruit and its liquid. Add an equal amount of sugar. Stir until sugar is dissolved, microwave on high for 5-10 minutes or until marmalade forms a gel. Test by placing a teaspoon of marmalade onto a saucer, place in the freezer for a few minutes. If ready, the surface of the marmalade will wrinkle when touched lightly.

Nutritional information/tablespoon: 0 g fat, 0.5 g fibre, 175 kJ.

1 lemon
2 oranges
1 grapefruit
Sugar

BANANA SMOOOTHIE

1 Place all ingredients in blender, process until smooth and frothy.

Ideal for a quick breakfast when you are running late.

Nutritional information/serving: 2.5 g fat, 3.5 g fibre, 1165 kJ.

Serves 1

1 banana
½ cup low-fat natural yoghurt
½ cup low-fat milk
1 teaspoon of honey
2 teaspoons wheatgerm
2 ice blocks

soups

Soups are a boon for busy people because it is so easy to make several days' supply in one go. You can keep them in the refrigerator or freezer until required.

Hot steaming soups are great in winter, chilled soups are refreshing in summer. Add some good quality rye or wholemeal bread or a crusty roll, perhaps some fruit, salad or a little cheese, and you have a complete, easy meal.

POTATO AND LEEK SOUP

1 In a large saucepan, heat olive oil and gently cook leeks and garlic for 5 minutes without browning.

2 Add rosemary, potatoes and stock, bring to the boil, cover and simmer for 15 minutes, or until potatoes are tender.

3 Stir in lemon juice and pepper and ladle into warm bowls. Swirl yoghurt on top.

Potatoes rate as the most filling food and are, therefore, ideal for those wanting to slim.

Variation To make a smooth, creamy-tasting soup, place cooked mixture into blender and process until smooth.

Nutritional information/serving: 6 g fat, 6.5 g fibre, 115 kJ.

Serves 4

1 tablespoon olive oil

2 large leeks, washed thoroughly and sliced finely

2 cloves garlic

3 or 4 sprigs fresh rosemary

1 kg potatoes, peeled and cubed

4 cups chicken stock

2 tablespoons lemon juice

Freshly ground pepper

1 cup non-fat yoghurt

CHILLED AVOCADO SOUP

1 Peel avocado and remove stone. Place in blender with remaining ingredients and process until smooth. Cover and chill for about 30 minutes (or place in freezer for about 10 minutes). Garnish each serving with a sprig of fresh mint.

Not suitable to freeze or refrigerate for longer than a few hours.

This quick and easy recipe can be prepared in just a few minutes. Avocado has some fat but it is mostly healthy monounsaturated fat and comes with a range of valuable antioxidants.

Nutritional information/serving: 20 g fat, 1 g fibre, 985 kJ.

Serves 4

1 large ripe avocado
3 cups cold chicken stock
¼ cup lime juice

1 teaspoon grated lime rind
250 g low-fat natural yoghurt
4 sprigs fresh mint for garnish

Handy Hint
For creamy tasting, low-fat soups, add concentrated skim milk made by dissolving skim milk powder in a small amount of water. Add to soup just before serving.

16

CHILLED PEAR AND PLUM SOUP

1 Reserve 2 tablespoons plum juice. Slice pears and place into a saucepan. Add plums and the rest of their juice, lemon rind, cinnamon stick, cardamom and wine. Cover, bring to the boil and simmer gently for 10 minutes. Remove cinnamon stick.

2 Blend cornflour with reserved juice and stir into hot mixture. Simmer for 2 minutes.

3 Cool soup then purée in blender or food processor until smooth. Chill.

4 Serve topped with yoghurt.

Not suitable to freeze.

Another quick and easy soup which is delicious for brunch or lunch on a hot summer day. It is low in fat and kilojoules.

Nutritional information/serving: 0.5 g fat, 7 g fibre, 1496 kJ.

Serves 4

6 pears, peeled and cored
800 g can dark plums, stones removed
1 teaspoon finely grated lemon rind
1 cinnamon stick

Pinch cardamom powder
1 cup white wine
1 tablespoon cornflour
200 g low-fat natural yoghurt for garnish

Handy Hint
Soups made without salt need a good stock plus herbs and spices to provide flavour.

PUMPKIN SOUP

1 Preheat oven to 180°C. Cut pumpkin into large chunks and remove seeds. Place on a flat baking dish and bake in preheated oven for about 1 hour or until flesh is tender. When cool enough to handle, peel away and discard skin.

Roasting the pumpkin gives this soup a wonderful flavour. With crusty bread and a salad, it makes a complete and easy-to-prepare meal.

2 Heat olive oil in a large saucepan and gently sauté onion until soft but not brown. Add thyme, orange rind and stock, bring to the boil, cover and simmer for 15 minutes.

3 Remove piece of orange rind. Add pumpkin and simmer for a further 5 minutes.

4 Blend soup in batches in food processor or blender, adding skim milk powder and nutmeg. Return to saucepan, heat and serve. If desired, top each serving with a dollop of yoghurt and swirl with a fork. Garnish with a sprig of thyme.

Can be frozen.

Nutritional information/serving: 4.5 g fat, 3.5 g fibre, 710 kJ.

Serves 6		
1.5 kg pumpkin	4 cups chicken stock	
1 tablespoon olive oil	½ cup skim milk powder	
1 medium onion, chopped	Pinch nutmeg	
1 teaspoon dried thyme or 1 tablespoon fresh thyme	Yoghurt for garnish (optional)	
Piece of orange rind	Sprigs of thyme for garnish	

Handy Hint

To make chicken stock: Either keep the bones from a chicken meal or buy stock bones from a chicken shop. Place them in a large saucepan, add a bay leaf, 6 peppercorns, 2 sprigs of parsley and 1 roughly chopped carrot. Bring to the boil, cover and simmer for about 1 hour. Strain off stock, refrigerate and remove any fat. If desired, freeze stock in small portions.

FRESH TOMATO SOUP

1 Heat oil and gently cook onion and garlic until soft but not brown.

2 Add tomatoes, stock, wine, bay leaves and mint and simmer for 15 minutes. Remove bay leaf and mint.

3 Using a food processor or blender, purée soup. Just before serving stir in basil. Serve hot or chilled with a swirl of yoghurt, if desired.

Microwave Follow the instructions above, using a microsafe dish and cooking onion on high for 2-3 minutes and total mixture for approximately 10 minutes.

Variations
1 To make a Creamy Tomato Soup, when blending the soup, add 1 cup skim milk powder. Omit yoghurt.
2 Zucchini Soup, substitute 1 kg zucchini for the tomatoes. Add ½ teaspoon dried thyme or 2 teaspoons fresh thyme.
3 Cauliflower Soup, use fresh tarragon (if available) in place of basil. Blend mixture with 1 cup of skim milk powder. Omit yoghurt.

Nutritional information/serving: 5.5 g fat, 3.5 g fibre, 430 kJ.

Serves 4	
1 tablespoon olive oil	½ litre chicken stock
1 medium onion, finely chopped	2 bay leaves
1 clove garlic, crushed	2-3 sprigs of mint
1 kg very ripe tomatoes, skinned and roughly chopped*	2 tablespoons torn fresh basil
	Low-fat natural yoghurt for garnish (optional)

*A large can of tomatoes (preferably with no added salt) can be used in place of the fresh tomatoes but the flavour will not be as good.

BEETROOT SOUP

1 Heat oil in a medium saucepan using very gentle heat. Cook onion for 2-3 minutes until softened but not brown.

This recipe is easy to make, especially with a food processor. Serve it chilled on a hot day. It is low in fat and kilojoules and high in dietary fibre.

2 Add beetroot, apple, cabbage, stock, tomato purée, red wine and bay leaves. Bring to the boil, cover and simmer for 20 minutes. Remove bay leaves. Just before serving, add lemon juice and freshly ground pepper. Serve hot or chilled. Top each serve with a dollop of yoghurt and swirl with a fork to produce a striped effect. Sprinkle with parsley.

Microwave Cook onion with oil on high for 2 minutes. Add remaining ingredients and cook on high for 15 minutes.

Not suitable to freeze but can be kept, covered, in the refrigerator for several days.

Nutritional information/serving: 3 g fat, 6.5 g fibre, 635 kJ.

Serves 4

1 tablespoon olive oil
1 medium onion, chopped
4 beetroot, peeled and grated*
1 large apple, peeled, cored and sliced
1 cup shredded red cabbage
4 cups chicken stock
2 tablespoons tomato purée (no added salt)

½ cup red wine
3 bay leaves
2 tablespoons lemon juice
Freshly ground pepper
Low-fat natural yoghurt for garnish
2 tablespoons chopped parsley

If fresh beetroot are unavailable, use a large can of beetroot, including liquid (preferably no added salt).

21

SEAFOOD SOUP

1 In a large saucepan, place fish trimmings, prawn shells, water, carrot, wine, parsley, tarragon and lemon peel. Bring to the boil, cover and simmer for 20 minutes. Strain fish stock and set aside.

This soup is a complete meal, ideal for a special occasion. Ask at fish markets or fish shops for bones for making fish stock. If unavailable, use water. This soup is low in fat and kilojoules.

2 Heat oil in a large saucepan and gently sauté onion and garlic until softened, but not brown.

3 Add potatoes, leek and fish stock, bring to the boil, cover and simmer for 20 minutes. Purée in blender or food processor. Return to saucepan and reheat.

4 Add fish, simmer for 3 minutes and then add scallops and prawns and cook only until prawns are pink. Serve at once, in large bowls, garnished with dill or parsley and lemon.

This recipe is not suitable to microwave or freeze. It can be kept, covered, in the refrigerator for 1-2 days.

Variation Use any seafoods available. Mussels, baby squid or crab can be added or can replace prawns. Or use more fish and omit the shellfish. If using oysters, add just before serving, as they become tough if boiled.

Nutritional information/serving: 5.5 g fat, 2.5 g fibre, 865 kJ.

Serves 6

For fish stock:
750 g fish bones, trimmings or fish head
Shells from prawns
1.5 litres cold water
1 carrot, sliced
1 cup white wine
Few sprigs parsley
Few sprigs tarragon or ½ teaspoon dried tarragon leaves
Piece of lemon peel

For soup:
1 tablespoon olive oil
1 medium onion, sliced
2 cloves garlic, crushed
500 g potatoes, peeled and sliced
1 leek, cleaned and sliced
300 g boneless fish fillets
300 g scallops
200 g green prawns, peeled and deveined
Freshly snipped dill or chopped parsley for garnish
6 lemon wedges

22

SILVERBEET, BACON AND GARLIC SOUP

1 In a large saucepan, place bacon, garlic and onion. Cover and allow to sweat over a gentle heat until bacon is cooked.

This unpopular vegetable is more likely to be loved when served as a soup.

2 Shred spinach and add to bacon, along with stock. Bring to the boil, cover and simmer for about 10 minutes, or until spinach is cooked.

3 Purée soup in blender, adding milk. Reheat until piping hot. Serve sprinkled with mint.

Nutritional information/serving: 3 5 g fat, 4 5 g fibre, 490 kJ.

Serves 4

2 rashers lean bacon, diced
2 cloves garlic
1 medium onion, diced
Large bunch silverbeet, washed and coarse stems removed

4 cups chicken stock
2 cups low-fat milk
Pepper
½ cup chopped fresh mint

Handy Hint
Always use ripe tomatoes to give a good rich flavour to soups.

LENTIL SOUP

1 In a large heavy-based saucepan, heat oil and gently cook cumin, coriander, chilli and onion for 3-4 minutes.

Lentils are very nutritious. Unlike most legumes, they need not be pre-soaked and will cook in about 20 minutes. This soup is low in fat and high in dietary fibre.

2 Add stock, carrot, celery, tomatoes, mushrooms, capsicum, lentils and wine. Bring to the boil, cover and simmer for 25 minutes. Serve into large bowls, topped with parsley.

Microwave Cook onion with oil on high for 2 minutes. Add remaining ingredients and cook on high for 15 minutes.

Can be frozen.

Nutritional information/serving: 4 g fat, 8.5 g fibre, 915 kJ.

Serves 6

1 tablespoon olive oil
1 teaspoon cumin powder
2 teaspoons coriander powder
1 teaspoon finely chopped chilli
1 large onion, peeled and finely chopped
6 cups stock or water
1 cup sliced carrot
½ cup sliced celery

750 g tomatoes, chopped roughly or 800 g can tomatoes (no added salt), chopped
1 cup sliced mushrooms
1 red capsicum, seeded and diced
250 g red lentils
¼ cup red wine
2 tablespoons chopped parsley

FARMHOUSE SOUP

1 Place chickpeas and water in a large saucepan. Bring to the boil, cover tightly, cook for 1 minute and then turn off heat. Leave to stand for 1 hour. (If leaving legumes for a longer period, place in refrigerator so that they do not ferment.)

> This is a great soup to make one day and reheat the next. It has lots of fibre and little fat.

2 Drain peas and add 6 cups fresh water. Bring to the boil, add shank, onion and herbs and simmer gently with lid on for 2 hours. Discard bay leaves and herbs.

3 Remove shank and separate meat from the bone, discard bone and place meat in a covered container in the refrigerator. If time permits, place soup in the refrigerator to allow fat to settle on the surface for easy removal.

4 Heat soup, add meat, carrots, potato, parsnip, leeks, tomato and brown rice. Simmer for 20 minutes.

5 Add broccoli and beans and cook for a further 10 minutes.

Can be frozen.

Variations
1 Use any vegetables you have on hand to replace those listed.
2 For a vegetarian soup, simply omit the veal shank.
3 Substitute buckwheat or wholemeal noodles for the rice.

Nutritional information/serving: 2.5 g fat, 9 g fibre, 975 kJ.

Serves 8

250 g chickpeas	½ cup sliced parsnip
6 cups water	1 cup sliced leeks
1 large veal shank, sawn into chunks	2 cups chopped tomatoes, fresh or canned (no
1 onion, sliced finely	added salt)
2 sprigs rosemary	¾ cup brown rice
2 bay leaves	½ cup tomato paste
3 large sprigs parsley	1 cup broccoli pieces
1 cup sliced carrots	1 cup sliced green beans, fresh or frozen
1 cup diced potato	

pasta, rice and grains

Foods made from grains are low in fat and high in healthy carbohydrates, dietary fibre, minerals and vitamins of the B group. Nutritionists are urging us all to eat more of them. Athletes and those who exercise should be especially careful to ensure they eat plenty of these important foods.

Contrary to popular belief, pasta, rice and grain foods are not fattening — although the sauces served with them sometimes are. As long as they are not served with buttery, creamy or oily accompaniments, even those who need to lose weight can include these important foods.

PASTA WITH SALMON

1 Cook pasta according to directions on packet, making sure not to overcook.

A quick and easy meal, made from ingredients you probably have on hand. Low in fat and high in complex carbohydrate.

2 While pasta is cooking, heat olive oil over a gentle heat and cook green onions for 1-2 minutes. Add juice, orange rind, ricotta, salmon, dill and pepper and stir until heated through.

3 Drain pasta and return to saucepan. Add salmon mixture and pine nuts. Toss until well combined.

Microwave Not suitable to cook in microwave but can be reheated for 10 minutes on high in microwave.

Nutritional information/serving: 14 g fat, 5.5 g fibre, 2170 kJ.

Serves 4

400 g dry spiral or penne pasta	150 g ricotta cheese
2 teaspoons olive oil	220 g can red salmon, drained and flaked
1 cup sliced green onions	1 tablespoon chopped fresh dill
2 tablespoons orange juice	Freshly ground black pepper
2 teaspoons of finely grated orange rind	1 tablespoon toasted pine nuts

VEGETARIAN LASAGNE

1 Heat oil and gently cook onion, garlic and oregano for 3-4 minutes or until onion is soft but not brown.

This delicious recipe is quick and easy to make when you don't have time to make a traditional lasagne. It is also low in fat.

2 Add eggplant, carrots, tomatoes and tomato paste. Bring to the boil and simmer, uncovered, for 20 minutes. Add mushrooms and simmer a further 5 minutes.

3 In a greased lasagne dish, place a layer of noodles (3 sheets) and ⅓ of the tomato mixture. Dot with ⅓ of the ricotta. Repeat layers of pasta, tomato mixture, ricotta, remaining pasta and ricotta. Sprinkle with parmesan cheese.

4 Preheat oven to 180°C. Bake in preheated oven for 35 minutes.

Microwave Not suitable to microwave but it can be prepared ahead and reheated on high for 10 minutes.

Nutritional information/serving: 14 g fat, 6.5 g fibre, 1330 kJ.

Serves 4

1 tablespoon olive oil
1 medium onion, sliced
2 cloves garlic, crushed
1 teaspoon dried oregano leaves or 1 tablespoon fresh chopped oregano
1 medium eggplant, cut into cubes
2 medium carrots, grated

840g can tomatoes (no added salt), drained*
2 tablespoons tomato paste, no added salt
2 cups sliced mushrooms
375 g ricotta cheese
9 sheets instant lasagne noodles
2 tablespoons grated parmesan cheese

* reserve juice for another recipe

29

PRAWN AND ORANGE PASTA

1 Cook pasta according to directions on packet, making sure not to overcook. Drain well and place into a large heated serving bowl.

A very quick meal which you can whip up in 15 minutes. Ideal for family or guests. Quantities can be doubled for extra people. No-one would guess that such a delicious dish has so little fat.

2 While pasta is cooking, steam peas and asparagus for 3 minutes. Add capsicum and prawns and steam for a further 2 minutes.

3 Toss vegetables, prawns and pine nuts with hot pasta. Heat orange juice and add to pasta. Garnish with orange segments and mint.

Nutritional information/serving: 3.5 g fat, 9 g fibre, 1915 kJ.

Serves 4

375 g pasta
1 cup snow peas (topped and tailed)
1 cup fresh asparagus cut into 3 cm lengths
1 red capsicum, seeded and cut into strips
12 green king prawns, peeled and deveined

1 tablespoon toasted pine nuts
½ cup orange juice
2 oranges, peeled and cut into segments
Fresh mint for garnish

FETTUCCINE CARBONARA

1 Cook pasta according to directions on packet, making sure not to overcook.

Pasta with carbonara sauce is usually high in fat. Try this low-fat version. With a tossed green salad, it's ideal for those times when you want a quick easy meal.

2 Meanwhile, heat olive oil and gently cook ham, onion and garlic until onion is soft.

3 Beat eggs and milk together.

4 Drain pasta and return to saucepan. Add ham and egg mixture. Stir over a low heat for a minute or two until set.

Nutritional information/serving: 7 g fat, 4.5 g fibre, 1695 kJ.

Serves 4

400 g dry fettuccine
2 teaspoons olive oil
125 g lean leg ham, diced
1 medium onion, chopped finely

2 cloves garlic, crushed
3 eggs
1 cup evaporated skim milk
Freshly ground pepper

Handy Hint

To prevent pasta sticking together while cooking, use a large volume of water, make sure it is boiling vigorously, and add pasta slowly so that it does not go off the boil. Stir occasionally while cooking.

SPAGHETTI WITH CHICKEN LIVERS

1 Cook pasta according to directions on packet, making sure not to overcook.

Chicken livers are very high in iron and other nutrients. They are often more popular than other types of liver but must not be overcooked or they toughen.

2 While pasta is cooking, heat olive oil in a heavy-based pan until hot. Add chicken livers and rosemary and brown quickly. Do not overcook or liver will toughen.

3 Add whisky to pan and ignite with a match.

4 When flames die down, add green onions, mushrooms and lemon juice. When mixture boils, serve over drained spaghetti.

Nutritional information/serving: 8.5 g fat, 5.5 g fibre, 1785 kJ.

Serves 4

400 g dry spaghetti
1 tablespoon olive oil
350 g chicken livers, cleaned and sliced
2 sprigs fresh rosemary (or ½ teaspoon dried)

2 tablespoons whisky
½ cup sliced green onions
1 cup sliced mushrooms
2 tablespoons lemon juice

PASTA WITH PESTO

1 Cook pasta according to directions on the packet, making sure not to overcook.

2 Place basil and garlic in food processor and process until finely chopped. Add oil, lemon juice, pine nuts and cheese and process to a thick paste.

3 Drain pasta, return to saucepan and add pesto. Toss well and serve at once in heated bowls.

The pesto sauce can be prepared and frozen until required.

Fresh basil is one of the delights of summer. Pesto is quick and easy to make and freezes well. Olive oil adds flavour and contributes a healthy kind of fat, plus a range of important antioxidants.

Variations
1 Use parsley instead of basil.
2 Use walnuts or pecans instead of pine nuts.

Nutritional information/serving: 21 g fat, 7.5 g fibre, 2190 kJ.

Serves 4

375 g dry spaghetti or fettuccine
2 cups fresh basil leaves
1 clove garlic
¼ cup olive oil

2 tablespoons lemon juice
2 tablespoons toasted pine nuts
2 tablespoons parmesan cheese

FRAGRANT RICE

1 Place oil and spices in a pan or saucepan with a tight-fitting lid and cook over a gentle heat for 2 minutes, stirring occasionally. Add onion and garlic and continue cooking for another 3-4 minutes, or until onion softens.

> This rice is so delicious that it can be simply served with steamed vegetables for a delicious low-fat meal. Also delicious with grilled chicken breast and steamed vegetables.

2 Add rice, stirring to coat grains with spice mixture. Pour in stock and wine, bring to the boil, turn heat to low, cover and cook for 25 minutes.

3 Add nuts and toss to combine.

Microwave Using a microsafe dish, heat spices in oil on high for 2 minutes. Add onion and garlic and cook on high for 2-3 minutes. Add rice and liquids, cover and cook on medium for 15-18 minutes. Add nuts and serve.

Variation Add 150 g tofu, which has been cut into cubes and browned in a non-stick pan.

Nutritional information/serving: 10 g fat, 3 g fibre, 1695 kJ.

Serves 4

1 tablespoon olive oil	1 medium onion, chopped finely
1 teaspoon ground cumin	1 clove garlic, crushed
4 cardamom pods	1½ cups rice
1 teaspoon cinnamon	2½ cups chicken stock
Pinch ground cloves	½ cup white wine
½ teaspoon finely chopped ginger	¼ cup slivered almonds, toasted

Handy Hint

The best way to cook rice, barley or other grains is by the absorption method. Use 2 cups of water for every cup of grain. Bring to the boil, cover with a tight-fitting lid and simmer until water is absorbed. This takes about 15 minutes for white rice, 25-30 minutes for brown and 40 minutes for barley.

PASTA WITH SPRING VEGETABLES

1 Cook pasta according to directions on packet, making sure not to overcook.

Another low-fat, easy meal which you can prepare very quickly. Serve with some crusty bread and salad.

2 Steam broccoli, peas and beans for 3-5 minutes (they should still be crisp). Add capsicum and steam a further 2 minutes.

3 Drain pasta and toss with steamed vegetables, green onions, basil or parsley, mustard and yoghurt. Serve at once.

Microwave There is no advantage in cooking pasta in a microwave. The broccoli, peas and beans can be cooked, covered, in a microsafe dish without water on high for 4 minutes. Add capsicum and cook on high for another minute. The finished dish can be reheated, covered, for 10 minutes on high.

Variations
1 Add a bunch of fresh asparagus, cut into 4-5 cm lengths, with the broccoli.
2 Add a can of well-drained, flaked tuna.
3 Use a bunch of English spinach in place of broccoli and steam for 3-4 minutes, until barely wilted.

Nutritional information/serving: 2.5 g fat, 17 g fibre, 1815 kJ.

Serves 4

400 g spiral noodles
3 cups broccoli pieces
2 cups snow peas, topped and tailed
2 cups stringless green beans, topped and tailed
1 red capsicum, seeded and cut into strips

½ cup sliced green onions
½ cup finely chopped fresh basil or parsley
1 tablespoon grainy mustard
2 tablespoons natural yoghurt

VEGETARIAN SPANISH RICE

1   Using a large wok or pan, heat oil and gently cook onion, garlic and chilli for 3-4 minutes. Add rice and stir over low-medium heat for 2-3 minutes.

This is an easy healthy meal to serve when you have guests. If you have a microwave, you can have the dish ready to the last stage. A few minutes on high in the microwave, and your meal is ready.

2   Add stock and saffron, bring to the boil, cover and simmer for 30 minutes until liquid is almost absorbed.

3   Gently stir in tomatoes and peas and continue cooking for 3-4 minutes.

4   Tip rice into a large ovenproof dish. Decorate top with capsicum, mushrooms and basil, cover and cook in a moderate oven for 10 minutes.

5   Just before serving, arrange eggs and olives on top and sprinkle with pepper and parsley.

Microwave   In a large microsafe dish, cook oil, onion, garlic and chilli on high for 3 minutes. Add rice, stock and saffron, stir, cover and cook on high for 5 minutes, then medium for 10 minutes. Add tomatoes and peas and cook on medium for another 3 minutes. Decorate top of rice with capsicum, mushrooms and basil, cover and cook on medium for 3-4 minutes.

Nutritional information/serving: 9.5 g fat, 8.5 g fibre, 1850 kJ.

Serves 4

1 tablespoon olive oil	1 red capsicum, seeded and sliced
1 large purple onion, sliced	1 green capsicum, seeded and sliced
2 cloves garlic, crushed	2 cups sliced button mushrooms
1 teaspoon chopped chilli	1 tablespoon chopped fresh basil or 1 teaspoon
1½ cups long grain rice	dried
2½ cups chicken or vegetable stock	2-3 hard boiled eggs, cut into quarters
Pinch saffron dissolved in 2 teaspoons water	About 12 black olives
1½ cups chopped fresh tomatoes	Freshly ground pepper
1 cup frozen peas	½ cup chopped parsley

CRACKED WHEAT LOAF

1 Place wheat into a small saucepan or basin with a tight-fitting lid. Add boiling water, cover and stand for 10 minutes (wheat will absorb the water).

This loaf is delicious served hot with steamed vegetables or cold on sandwiches or with salads. It is high in dietary fibre and nutrients.

2 Meanwhile, heat oil and gently cook onion for 3-4 minutes or until softened but not brown.

3 Preheat oven to 180°C. Combine eggs, carrot, cottage cheese, wheatgerm, parsley, nuts and sesame seeds. Add wheat and onions and stir well. Press mixture into a greased loaf tin and bake in preheated oven for 40 minutes. Stand 5 minutes before turning out. Serve hot or cold.

Microwave Combine wheat and boiling water, as above. In a microsafe dish, cook oil and onion on high for 2-3 minutes. Add remaining ingredients. Pack into a greased microsafe loaf dish and cook on medium for 15-20 minutes. Stand 5 minutes before turning out.

Nutritional information/serving: 22 g fat, 6 g fibre, 1430 kJ.

Serves 6

1 cup cracked wheat	1 cup cottage cheese
2 cups boiling water	½ cup wheatgerm
1 tablespoon olive oil	½ cup chopped parsley
1 medium onion, finely chopped	1 cup pecan nuts or walnut pieces, roughly chopped
2 eggs, beaten	1 tablespoon toasted sesame seeds
1 carrot, grated	

Handy Hint
Burghul or cracked wheat has already been partly steamed. It should be covered with boiling water, covered tightly and left to stand for 10-15 minutes, until all the water is absorbed. Use 2 cups of boiling water to 1 cup of cracked wheat.

RICE-STUFFED TOMATOES

1 Cut tops off tomatoes, carefully scoop out flesh and turn tomato shells upside down to drain well.

Stuffed tomatoes are quick, easy and nutritious. They make a great lunch, brunch or main meal dish. They are low in fat and kilojoules.

2 Preheat oven to 180°C. Combine rice, basil, cottage cheese and egg. Fill tomato shells with mixture, then sprinkle with crumbs and cheese. Bake in preheated oven for 15 minutes. Serve with steamed vegetables or salad and/or grilled fish or chicken.

Microwave Cook tomatoes, uncovered, in microwave on high for 5 minutes.

Variations
1 Instead of rice, use cooked burghul.
2 Instead of rice, use cooked barley.
3 For stuffed capsicums, halve capsicums, remove seeds. Fill with stuffing mixture and cook as for the tomatoes, allowing an extra 5 minutes, if necessary.

Nutritional information/serving: 6 g fat, 3.5 g fibre, 775 kJ.

Serves 4

4 large tomatoes
1 cup cooked brown rice
2 tablespoons chopped fresh basil leaves
¼ cup cottage cheese

1 egg, beaten
1 slice bread, made into crumbs
1 tablespoon grated cheese

BARLEY AND MUSHROOM CASSEROLE

1 Heat oil and gently cook onion without browning for 3-4 minutes. Add barley and stir well. Add sliced mushrooms, stock and thyme. Cover with a tight-fitting lid and cook over a low heat for 45 minutes.

> Grains and mushrooms make a good combination. This is a great dish on its own, accompanied by lightly steamed vegetables or salad or with chicken.

2 Add remaining mushrooms to barley and continue cooking for a further 5 minutes. The barley should be tender and all liquid should be absorbed.

Microwave Place oil and onion in a microsafe dish, and cook on high for 2-3 minutes. Add barley, sliced mushrooms, stock and thyme, cover and cook on high for 5 minutes, then on medium for 25 minutes. Add mushrooms and cook on high for 3 minutes.

Variations
1 Use brown rice in place of the barley. Reduce cooking time to 35 minutes before adding remaining mushrooms.
2 Add ½ cup toasted pecan nuts with the button mushrooms.

Nutritional information/serving: 11 g fat, 9.5 g fibre, 1200 kJ.

Serves 2

1 tablespoon olive oil	1 cup chicken stock
1 small onion, finely chopped	½ teaspoon dried thyme or 1 tablespoon fresh
½ cup barley	chopped thyme
100 g button mushrooms, sliced	12 small whole button mushrooms

BARLEY BUNS

1 Place barley and water in a small saucepan with a tight-fitting lid. Bring to the boil, cover and simmer for 40 minutes, or until water is absorbed.

Barley is a highly nutritious product with a high level of soluble fibre. Try this recipe for a delightful lunch or evening meal.

2 Heat oil and gently cook onion, without browning. Add mushrooms and sauté for 1-2 minutes.

3 Combine parsley, thyme, egg and cottage cheese. Add onion, mushrooms and barley and mix well to combine all ingredients.

4 Cut a slice from the top of each roll and carefully pull out the insides. Using blender or food processor, make into crumbs and add to barley mixture.

5 Preheat oven to 180°C. Fill rolls with stuffing, packing mixture in well. Sprinkle with parmesan, replace slices cut from tops and bake in preheated oven for 10-15 minutes or until rolls are crisp.

Nutritional information/serving: 14 g fat, 7.5 g fibre, 1650 kJ.

Serves 4

½ cup barley	1 teaspoon dried thyme or 1 tablespoon fresh thyme leaves
1 cup water	1 egg, lightly beaten
1 tablespoon olive oil	¾ cup cottage cheese
1 medium onion, chopped finely	4 wholemeal bread rolls
125 g mushrooms, chopped	1 tablespoon grated parmesan
2 tablespoons finely chopped parsley	

RICE PIE CRUST

1 Preheat oven to 180°C. Combine all ingredients and press into a greased 22 cm pie dish. Bake in preheated oven for 15 minutes.

Faster and easier to cook than pastry and much more nutritious.

Nutritional information: 1/6 pie crust – 2 g fat, 1 g fibre, 455 kJ.

2 cups cooked rice (brown or white)
1 egg, beaten
1 tablespoon chopped parsley or mint

1 tablespoon lemon juice
1 tablespoon toasted sesame seeds

Handy Hint
Pasta should be cooked so that it is 'al dente' (literally 'to the tooth'). Taste test so that you do not overcook it.

TUNA RICE PIE

1 Combine flaked, drained tuna with green onions, mushrooms and celery. Place into pie crust.

A fast, easy, low-fat recipe. Serve it with a crisp salad.

2 Beat eggs and milk, add thyme and pour mixture over tuna. Bake at 180°C for 30 minutes.

Nutritional information/serving: 5.5 g fat, 2 g fibre, 995 kJ.

Serves 6

1 rice pie crust, baked (recipe above)
400 g can tuna (no added salt), drained
¼ cup sliced green onions
200 g mushrooms, sliced
½ cup sliced celery

1 cup evaporated skim milk
2 eggs
½ teaspoon dried thyme or 1 tablespoon fresh thyme

BARLEY-STUFFED CAPSICUMS

1 In a saucepan, heat water, barley and onion, cover, simmer over low heat for 40 minutes.

Barley is so nutritious, it should be used more. If you have never tried it before, give it a go.

2 Combine cooked barley with mushrooms, ricotta cheese, egg and parsley.

3 Preheat oven to 180°C. Fill capsicum halves with barley mixture and top with cheese. Bake for 20 minutes. Serve with steamed vegetables or salad.

Microwave Cook water, barley and onion in a microsafe dish, covered, on high for 20 minutes. Combine with mushrooms, ricotta cheese, egg and parsley. Fill capsicum shells and cook, uncovered, on high for 10 minutes. Top with cheese, cook on high for 1 minute.

Nutritional information/serving: 13 g fat, 7 g fibre, 1445 kJ.

Serves 4

1 cup barley
2 cups water
1 medium onion, chopped finely
1 cup mushrooms, sliced
¾ cup ricotta cheese

1 egg, beaten
2 tablespoons chopped fresh parsley
2 large red capsicums, cut in half lengthwise and seeds removed
4 slices Swiss cheese

seafood

The more we learn about nutrition, the more we realise the value of fish in the diet. Most fish contain very little fat, but what is present contains valuable omega 3 fatty acids. These help stop blood clots forming and may also regulate inflammatory reactions within the body.

The widespread idea that shellfish should be avoided by those with high cholesterol levels is not valid. Most of the cholesterol in the blood comes from saturated fats in foods; all seafoods are low in saturated fats, unless battered or crumbed and fried in fat. Oysters are a great food for those with high cholesterol and prawns can also be included quite safely. I have also included recipes for canned tuna and salmon which are both handy and nutritious products.

ROSEMARY FISH

1 Cut 4 squares of foil, approximately 25-30 cm square. On each piece of foil, place a sprig of rosemary and a slice of lemon. Top with a fish cutlet

and remaining rosemary and lemon. Sprinkle each with 1 tablespoon of wine. Fold foil parcels so that fish is completely enclosed and cook on barbecue for 15-20 minutes, turning once. If desired, fish parcels can also be baked at 180°C for 20 minutes.

2 In a small saucepan, heat lemon juice and remaining wine until boiling. Blend cornflour with water and stir into a sauce until mixture thickens. Simmer for 1 minute. To serve, open foil parcels, remove fish from foil and top each fillet with a little of the sauce.

Microwave Use baking paper instead of foil. Cook on high for 5-6 minutes. Remove from microwave. Heat wine and lemon juice on high for 2 minutes, blend cornflour with water, add to sauce and heat on medium for 1-2 minutes.

Nutritional information/serving: 4.5 g fat, 1 g fibre, 890 kJ.

Serves 4

4 fish cutlets (kingfish, blue-eye cod or other fish)	½ cup lemon juice
8 small sprigs fresh rosemary	1 teaspoon cornflour
1 lemon, cut into 8 slices	1 tablespoon water
¾ cup white wine	

Handy Hint
Fresh fish fillets should look shiny and firm. Reject any which are discoloured or have water oozing out of them. Whole fish should have bright eyes which have not become sunken.

SESAME HERBED TUNA STEAKS

1 Place sesame seeds in a non-stick pan and heat gently until golden brown. Tip onto a flat plate. Add herbs and pepper. Dip tuna steaks into sesame mixture, turning so that the mixture sticks to both sides of the tuna.

A simple way to cook this superb fish. Be careful not to overcook tuna or it will be dry.

2 Heat non-stick pan and add tuna. Cook for no more than 3-4 minutes on each side. Sprinkle with lemon juice and serve at once.

Delicious served with a salad of Pasta with Pesto (see page 35) and sliced ripe red tomatoes.

Nutritional information/serving: 8 g fat, 0.5 g fibre, 865 kJ.

Serves 4

1 tablespoon sesame seeds
2 teaspoons dried salad herbs
½ teaspoon coarsely ground black pepper

4 tuna steaks, about 125-150 g each
1 tablespoon lemon juice

BAKED WHOLE BREAM

1 Make 3 cuts in the thickest part of each fish. Place a sprig of lemon thyme into each.

An ideal low-fat meal for two. Increase the quantities to serve more people.

2 Combine lemon juice, rind, peppercorns and thyme. Rub over skin of fish, allowing some to lodge in cuts.

3 Preheat oven to 180°C. Place fish in lightly greased ovenproof dish. Cover lightly with foil. Bake in preheated oven for 15-20 minutes, or until fish flakes easily with a fork.

Microwave Remove heads from fish. Proceed as above, covering fish loosely with microsafe plastic wrap. Cook on medium for 10-12 minutes, or until flesh flakes easily.

Nutritional information/serving: 10 g fat, 0 g fibre, 1070 kJ.

Serves 2

2 sea bream, each about 400 g
6 sprigs lemon thyme or thyme
2 tablespoons lemon juice
1 teaspoon grated lemon rind

1 teaspoon green peppercorns
½ teaspoon dried thyme leaves or 2 teaspoons fresh thyme leaves

Handy Hint

If you don't like the smell of fish cooking (or washing fishy dishes afterwards), wrap fish in foil (shiny side in) and bake or barbecue. This retains both moisture and flavour. Or use your microwave.

BARBECUED OCEAN TROUT

1 Combine all marinade ingredients. Place fish into marinade and leave in refrigerator for at least 1 hour, or cover and refrigerate for up to 24 hours.

Fish is one of the easiest foods to cook on a barbecue. A marinade enhances the flavour.

2 Remove fish from marinade, place on hot barbecue plate and cook until fish flakes easily, about 3-5 minutes.

Fish can also be cooked in microwave on high for 5-6 minutes.

Variations Other thick-fleshed fish (such as gemfish, flounder, ocean perch, kingfish, blue-eye cod) can be used in place of ocean trout. This dish can also be cooked under a hot griller. Line griller with foil, cook until flesh flakes but be careful not to overcook. There is no need to turn fish.

Nutritional information/serving: 19 g fat, 0 g fibre, 1300 kJ

Serves 4

4 fillets or cutlets of ocean trout, about 750 g

Marinade:
1 cup white wine
1 tablespoon olive oil
2 teaspoons dried parsley or 1 tablespoon chopped fresh parsley
2 teaspoons mixed herbs such as thyme, rosemary, oregano or 2 tablespoons fresh herbs
Coarsely cracked pepper to taste
2 tablespoons lemon juice

STIR-FRIED FISH WITH MUSHROOMS

1 In a wok or large frying pan, heat oil and gently cook onion for 2-3 minutes, or until softened. Add ginger, fish and vegetables and stir-fry for 2-3 minutes.

2 Add mushrooms, tossing gently to heat.

3 Combine coconut milk, soy sauce and lime or lemon juice. Pour into wok and stir gently until boiling.

4 Blend cornflour and water and stir into mixture. Simmer 1 minute. Serve with steamed rice.

A healthy low-fat, high-fibre meal which can be prepared quickly. Place rice on to cook while preparing the fish.

Nutritional information/serving: 10 g fat, 2.5 g fibre, 800 kJ.

Serves 6

1 tablespoon macadamia nut oil
1 medium onion, sliced
2 teaspoons finely chopped fresh ginger
500 g boneless fish fillets, cut into strips
2 cups mixed sliced vegetables (broccoli, cauliflower, celery, capsicum, carrot, zucchini)

250 g sliced button mushrooms
½ cup coconut milk
1 tablespoon salt-reduced soy sauce
2 tablespoons lime or lemon juice
2 teaspoons cornflour
2 tablespoons water

MEDITERRANEAN FISH CASSEROLE

1 In a large wok or deep frypan, heat oil and gently cook onion and garlic for 2-3 minutes, without browning.

> **If you've never made a fish casserole, this one is easy and healthy. Serve with tiny steamed new potatoes and a green vegetable.**

2 Add tomatoes, eggplant, wine, bay leaves and peppercorns, bring to the boil and simmer for 10 minutes.

3 Add fish and continue cooking for a further 5 minutes, or until fish fillets flake easily with a fork. Add lemon juice, basil and olives. Remove bay leaves before serving.

Microwave Place oil, onion and garlic into a microsafe dish and cook on high for 2 minutes. Add tomatoes, eggplant, wine, bay leaves and peppercorns and cook on high for 5-6 minutes. Add fish and cook on high for 5 minutes. Add remaining ingredients.

Nutritional information/serving: 9 g fat, 3.5 g fibre, 1090 kJ.

Serves 4	1 tablespoon olive oil
	1 medium onion, sliced
	1 clove garlic, crushed
	500 g tomatoes, peeled and chopped
	1 cup cubed eggplant
	1 cup white wine

2 bay leaves
1 tablespoon pink peppercorns
500 g boneless fish fillets, cut into 3 cm cubes
1 tablespoon lemon juice
2 tablespoons torn basil leaves
12 black olives

57

FISH ROULADES

1 Steam spinach for 2 minutes. Spread spinach onto a clean tea-towel to absorb water.

When you want something a little special, try this recipe.

2 Heat oil in a heavy-based pan and brown bread cubes and pine nuts, stirring often.

3 Preheat oven to 180°C. Combine egg, dill, lemon rind, bread and pine nuts. Place 4 spinach leaves onto each fish fillet and top with one quarter of the bread mixture. Roll up and secure with toothpicks. Place roulades into a greased, shallow casserole just large enough to hold them. Cover and bake in preheated oven for 20-25 minutes.

4 Place strips of lemon rind in a small saucepan, cover with water, bring to the boil and simmer for 2 minutes. Drain. When fish is cooked, garnish with lemon rind and dill.

Microwave Cook fish fillets on high for 7-8 minutes.

Nutritional information/serving: 11 g fat, 5 g fibre, 1210 kJ.

Serves 4

4 thin fillets of gemfish or other white-fleshed fish
16 leaves English spinach
1 tablespoon olive oil
3 slices wholemeal bread, crusts removed and cut into 1 cm squares

1 tablespoon pine nuts
1 egg, beaten
Fine strips of lemon rind
1 tablespoon chopped dill

58

SCALLOPS AND MUSHROOMS ON SKEWERS

Scallops:

1 Thread scallops, mushrooms, capsicum and water chestnuts onto skewers. Sprinkle scallops with lemon juice.

This is an easy method for cooking scallops. For a special occasion, add red capsicum sauce. Skinning capsicums removes any bitterness and the sweet puréed flesh enhances the scallops.

2 Grill over hot coals on barbecue or under griller for 3-4 minutes, turning frequently. Serve with steamed rice and red capsicum sauce.

Red Capsicum Sauce:

1 Place capsicum onto a long fork or metal skewer and hold over a gas flame until skin is blackened. Place in a brown paper bag for 10 minutes. When cool enough to handle, peel away blackened skin, catching any juices.

2 Place capsicum into blender or food processor with olive oil and purée until smooth. Add pepper to taste.

Nutritional information/serving: *Scallops* – 1 g fat, 2.5 g fibre, 445 kJ.
Sauce – 5 g fat, 1 g fibre, 270 kJ.

Serves 4

500 g Tasmanian scallops
Small can water chestnuts, drained and cut in halves
12 button mushrooms
1 capsicum, red or green, seeded and cut into 2.5 cm squares
Bamboo skewers, soaked in water to prevent burning
1 tablespoon lemon juice

Red Capsicum Sauce:
2 red capsicums
1 tablespoon olive oil
freshly ground pepper

60

BARBECUED OCTOPUS

1 Remove octopus heads. Cut out small 'beak' in centre of tentacles and halve each octopus.

> Octopus is easy to cook but make sure your fishmonger has fresh octopus and don't overcook, otherwise they will be too tough.

2 Combine oil, wine, garlic and oregano. Place octopus into marinade and refrigerate for at least 15 minutes.

3 Remove octopus from marinade. Have barbecue very hot. Cook octopus for 6-8 minutes, brushing with marinade. Octopus will turn red and curl up slightly. Do not overcook or flesh will toughen. Serve with salad and plenty of crusty bread.

Nutritional information/serving (includes marinade): 16 g fat, 0.5 g fibre, 1020 kJ.

Serves 4

600 g small octopus
¼ cup olive oil
¼ cup red wine

2 cloves garlic, crushed
2 teaspoon dried oregano leaves or 1 tablespoon fresh oregano

Handy Hint
Fish is dry if overcooked. Fish fillets or cutlets usually take only 5-8 minutes to cook. Whole fish take longer, depending on the size of the fish. To test fish, insert a fork. If the flakes part easily, the fish is cooked.

SPICY PRAWNS

1 In a shallow dish, combine olive oil, sherry, soy sauce, honey, ginger and chilli.

One of the easiest barbecue dishes, prawns are best prepared simply. Serve with plenty of salads and crusty breads for an ideal Sunday lunch.

2 Thread prawns onto skewers and refrigerate in marinade mixture for at least 1 hour.

3 Sprinkle sesame seeds onto prawns and grill or barbecue for about 3 minutes, turning once and brushing with marinade mixture while cooking.

Nutritional information/serving: 10 g fat, 1.5 g fibre, 890 kJ.

Serves 4

1 tablespoon olive oil
½ cup sherry
1 tablespoon salt-reduced soy sauce
2 teaspoons honey
2 teaspoons minced fresh ginger

1 teaspoon chopped chilli
16 green king prawns, peeled and deveined with tails left on
¼ cup toasted sesame seeds
Bamboo skewers, soaked in water to prevent burning

Handy Hint

To split prawns before barbecuing them, use a pair of small scissors.

TUNA PASTITSIO

1 Combine onion, garlic, tomatoes, tomato paste, parsley and pepper. Add tuna, mix gently.

2 For sauce, blend flour with milk in food processor. Pour into a saucepan and cook over a low heat, stirring constantly, until thick. Mix in parmesan cheese and allow to cool a little. Stir in eggs and nutmeg.

3 Preheat oven to 180°C. Place a layer of lasagne noodles in a greased casserole, top with half the tuna mixture, another layer of lasagne noodles, remaining tuna and a third layer of noodles. Pour sauce over the top. Sprinkle with grated cheddar and paprika. Bake in preheated oven for 30 minutes.

Microwave Lasagne can be cooked in microwave on high for 20 minutes. Stand 10 minutes before serving.

Nutritional information/serving: 8 g fat, 3.5 g fibre, 1445 kJ.

Serves 6

1 medium onion, chopped finely
1 clove garlic, crushed
2 cups chopped tomatoes, fresh or canned
1 tablespoon tomato paste
2 tablespoons chopped parsley
Freshly ground pepper
425 g can tuna, no added salt, drained
2 cups skim milk

2 tablespoons plain flour
2 tablespoons grated parmesan cheese
2 eggs, beaten
Pinch nutmeg
250 g instant lasagne noodles
½ cup cheddar cheese, grated
½ teaspoon paprika

TUNA-STUFFED POTATOES

1 Preheat oven to 180°C. Prick potatoes with a skewer and bake in preheated oven for 1 hour, or until soft when pierced with a skewer.

Another easy, low-fat meal – very fast if you use a microwave, although not as delicious.

2 Cut 'lid' from potatoes, scoop out flesh, leaving a wall to support the potato. Mash potato flesh with a fork and combine with tuna, yoghurt, pepper, sprouts and oregano. Stuff mixture into potato shells, sprinkle with cheese and replace lids. Bake for a further 15 minutes.

Microwave Prick potatoes and cook in microwave on high for 12-15 minutes, or until tender when pierced with a fine skewer. Proceed as above. Reheat potatoes on high for 3-4 minutes.

Nutritional information/serving: 2.5 g fat, 4 g fibre, 995 kJ.

Serves 4

4 red-skinned potatoes, about 250 g each
200 g canned tuna, well drained
2 tablespoons low-fat yoghurt
½ teaspoon lemon pepper

½ cup mung bean sprouts
1 tablespoon fresh oregano or ½ teaspoon dried
1 tablespoon grated parmesan cheese

SALMON BURGERS

1 Combine salmon, ricotta, spring onions, parsley, zucchini, lemon juice, lemon rind and egg and mix well. Form into 4 patties.

2 Combine wheatgerm and sesame seeds. Roll patties in mixture. Place in refrigerator for 30 minutes.

3 Cook in a hot, non-stick pan for 10 minutes, turning once.

Serve in a toasted wholemeal bun with lettuce, tomato, beetroot and alfalfa sprouts.

Nutritional information/serving: 17 g fat, 3.5 g fibre, 1210 kJ.

Makes 4

400 g can pink salmon, drained	1 tablespoon lemon juice
1 cup ricotta cheese	1 teaspoon grated lemon rind
½ cup chopped spring onions	1 egg
2 tablespoons chopped dill or parsley	½ cup wheatgerm
1 medium zucchini, finely grated	2 tablespoons toasted sesame seeds

poultry
and meats

Chicken is one of the easiest foods to fit into a healthy diet. Most of the fat is in the skin and pads just beneath it. Once these are removed, the flesh is low in fat. Skinless chicken legs, thighs and breasts are now available.

Turkey, veal and lean cuts of pork are also low in fat. If you are going to crumb and fry these meats, however, you might as well settle for a fatty steak. In this chapter you'll find some new ideas. Some cuts of beef and lamb can also be very lean. Trim all fat before cooking.

BARBECUED TIPSY CHICKEN

1 Combine juice, brandy and marmalade, add chicken, turning several times to coat with marinade. Cover and refrigerate for at least 1 hour, or overnight.

2 Remove chicken from marinade and place on a heated barbecue. Cook for about 15 minutes, turning several times and brushing with marinade.

Serve with potatoes which have been steamed and mashed, or with steamed new potatoes, salad or vegetables.

Nutritional information/serving: 4 g fat, 0 g fibre, 1100 kJ.

Serves 4	4 skinless chicken breast fillets, about 700 g	2 tablespoons brandy
	½ cup lime or lemon juice	2 tablespoons orange marmalade

Handy Hint
To stop chicken sticking to barbecue, place it into microwave and cook on high for 5 minutes. Then remove chicken pieces from microwave and barbecue.

SPICY PEANUT DRUMSTICKS

1 Combine onion, garlic, spice, stock, peanut butter and tomatoes in a saucepan. Stir over a moderate heat for 5 minutes.

A popular meal with children as well as adults. It's also great for parties.

2 Preheat oven to 180°C. Arrange drumsticks in a shallow ovenproof dish and top with mushrooms. Pour sauce over chicken. Bake in oven for 30-40 minutes, or until chicken is tender. Serve with steamed basmati rice and salad.

Microwave In a microsafe dish, combine onion, garlic, spice, stock, peanut butter and tomatoes. Cover and cook on high for 5 minutes, stirring once or twice. Add drumsticks and mushrooms, cover loosely and microwave on high for 12 minutes, or until drumsticks are tender.

Nutritional information/serving: 27 g fat, 7 g fibre, 1790 kJ.

Serves 4

8 chicken drumsticks
1 onion, sliced
1 clove garlic, crushed
2 teaspoons garam marsala spice
1 cup chicken stock

½ cup crunchy peanut butter, no added salt
1 tablespoon salt-reduced soy sauce
2 large tomatoes, peeled and chopped
150 g mushrooms, sliced

70

CHICKEN WITH CAMEMBERT

1 Remove any fatty pads from chicken. Place camembert and herbs inside chicken.

2 Bake at 180°C for 1½ hours, or until tender. Serve with steamed new potatoes, lightly cooked vegetables and/or salad.

The camembert melts and gives a delightful creamy flavour. It adds 9 grams of fat to each serve, but is so simple and delicious that I suggest you skip some other source of fat that day so that you can fit it into your healthy diet.

Nutritional information/serving (without skin): 16 g fat, 0 g fibre, 1290 kJ.

Serves 4   1 x No. 14 chicken   2 tablespoons fresh lemon thyme or chopped fresh
           125 g camembert cheese   rosemary or parsley

SPICY BARBECUED CHICKEN

1 Combine yoghurt, spices, chilli, ginger and lemon juice.

> This recipe has very little fat, is quick to prepare and is deliciously different. Serve it at your next barbecue or cook it in the kitchen oven.

2 Place chicken breasts in a shallow dish, pour yoghurt mixture over, turning chicken to coat. Cover and refrigerate for at least 3 hours, or overnight.

3 Remove chicken from marinade and grill on a rack over hot coals, turning several times and brushing with marinade for 20-30 minutes, or until tender.

Alternatively, bake chicken and marinade in an open ovenproof dish at 180°C for 40 minutes. The yoghurt will separate during cooking, but the flavour is superb.

Serve with crusty bread, steamed rice (preferably basmati) or Cracked Wheat Salad and a green salad.

Microwave Cook chicken (and yoghurt mixture) on medium for 7-9 minutes.

Nutritional information/serve: 3.5 g fat, 0 g fibre, 855 kJ.

Serves 4

1 cup low-fat natural yoghurt
2 teaspoons ground coriander
2 teaspoons garam masala
1 teaspoon ground cinnamon
1 teaspoon chopped fresh chilli (use more, if desired)

1 teaspoon finely chopped fresh ginger
2 tablespoons lemon juice
4 skinless chicken breasts, about 600 g

If you want, you can replace spices with ready-made tandoori spice mix.

Handy Hint

Chicken breasts now grill well without drying out. This is because the flesh is left on the bone for 24 hours, giving an effect similar to the ageing of steak.

STEAMED CHICKEN

1 Remove and discard fat from inside areas and tail of chicken. Place chicken into large saucepan and pour boiling water over. Leave for 1 minute, drain away water, remove chicken and pat dry.

> Steamed chicken is sometimes dry. This recipe produces a moist, succulent chicken. Eat it as it is or use the flesh for sandwiches, salads or in pasta or rice dishes.

2 Combine ginger, shallots, lemon juice, soy sauce, sesame oil and sherry and brush the mixture over the inside and outside of chicken.

3 Place chicken in steamer or use a steaming rack in a large saucepan. Steam over boiling water for 1 hour.

Nutritional information/serving (without skin): 10 g fat, 0 g fibre, 1050 kJ.

Serves 4	1 x No. 14 chicken	1 tablespoon lemon juice
	1.5 litres boiling water	1 tablespoon salt-reduced soy sauce
	2 teaspoons fresh ginger slices	2 teaspoons sesame oil
	¼ cup shallots, chopped finely	2 tablespoons dry sherry

Handy Hint

If you cannot resist the crisp brown fat on meat or the skin of chicken, cut it off before you cook it. Cold white lumps of fat don't tempt the tastebuds.

BASIL AND HAM-STUFFED CHICKEN THIGHS

1 Remove fat pads from chicken but leave skin intact.

A delightful, full flavoured dish. Lean leg ham has less fat than bacon.

2 In a small frypan, heat oil and cook ham and garlic over a low heat for 2-3 minutes. Add basil, lemon juice and nuts. Allow to cool.

3 Preheat oven to 180°C. Lift up skin on chicken and carefully push one quarter of the basil mixture under the skin of each thigh, working mixture down into the legs. Bake for 45 minutes.

Nutritional information/serving: 20 g fat, 1 g fibre, 1190 kJ.

Serves 4

4 chicken maryland pieces
2 teaspoons olive oil
50 g lean leg ham, finely chopped
1 clove garlic, crushed

1 cup torn fresh basil leaves
2 tablespoons lemon juice
1 tablespoon flaked almonds

THAI CHICKEN

1 Preheat oven to 200°C. Wrap shrimp paste in foil and bake in preheated oven for 10 minutes.

To save time in making this recipe, use prepared Thai seasoning in place of the chilli, onion, garlic, lemon grass, coriander, lemon juice and lime leaves. The coconut milk adds some fat, but there is no substitute for the flavour.

2 In a wok or large frying pan, place shrimp paste, chilli, onion, garlic, lemon grass, coriander and lemon or lime juice. Heat gently, stirring constantly and cook for 2-3 minutes. Add lime leaves and coconut milk and mix well.

3 Add chicken to coconut milk mixture, bring to the boil and simmer gently for 12-15 minutes, or until chicken is tender. Add fish sauce. Garnish with coriander.

Serve with rice and stir-fried snow peas.

Microwave Prepare sauce as above, cook on medium for 2 minutes. Add chicken, cover loosely and cook on medium for 10-12 minutes.

Nutritional information/serve: 18 g fat, 1 g fibre, 1200 kJ.

Serves 4

1 teaspoon dried shrimp paste
1 red chilli, seeded and chopped finely
1 medium onion, chopped
1 clove garlic, crushed
1 tablespoon lemon grass*, finely sliced
2 tablespoons fresh coriander roots, finely chopped
2 tablespoons lemon juice

1 tablespoon finely sliced kaffir lime leaves (or substitute young leaves from a lemon or lime tree)
1 cup coconut milk
500 g chicken tenderloin fillets, or breast fillets cut into strips
1 teaspoon Thai fish sauce
2 tablespoons fresh coriander

* Lemon grass is available in pots from nurseries or from Asian food stores.

76

CAJUN CHICKEN

1 Remove seeds from chilli and chop flesh finely, taking care to wash hands and all surfaces carefully afterwards. Combine chilli, peppercorns, sugar and lime juice. Spread mixture evenly over thigh fillets.

A spicy, simple and different meal.

2 Heat oil in a wok or frypan; add chicken and cook for 3-4 minutes. Turn and cook other side for 3-4 minutes, until done. Serve with rice and garnish with green onions and a dollop of yoghurt.

Microwave Heat oil in microsafe dish, add chicken and cook on high for 3-4 minutes, turn and cook another 3-4 minutes until done.

Nutritional information/serving: 17 g fat, 2 g fibre, 1750 kJ.

Serves 4
1 red chilli	8 skinless chicken thigh fillets
1 tablespoon crushed black peppercorns	1 tablespoon macadamia nut oil
2 tablespoons dark brown sugar	4 green onions, thinly sliced
2 tablespoons lime juice	200 g natural low-fat yoghurt

Handy Hint

For stir-fried dishes, freeze meat or chicken breast for 30 minutes or so before slicing. Using a sharp knife, it is then easy to slice the flesh very thinly. This helps the meat to cook quickly and stay tender.

CHICKEN AND RICOTTA ROULADES

1 Combine ricotta, parsley, lemon juice, chicken, mushrooms and peppercorns.

This dish is simple to prepare. Try it for a dinner party or any family meal.

2 Preheat oven to 200°C. Place 2 sheets of filo one on top of the other on bench, place a quarter of the chicken mixture on each sheet. Roll up pastry and seal by brushing with a little oil. Repeat with remaining filling and pastry. Brush surfaces with remaining oil. Bake for 30 minutes, or until golden brown.

Serve with steamed vegetables and/or a tossed salad.

Nutritional information/serving: 14 g fat, 2 g fibre, 1200 kJ.

Serves 4

1 cup ricotta cheese	250 g button mushrooms, sliced finely
1 tablespoon finely chopped parsley	1 tablespoon pink peppercorns
1 tablespoon lemon juice	8 sheets filo pastry
150 g cooked chicken, cut into small cubes	1 tablespoon olive oil

CHICKEN WITH HONEY CHILLI SAUCE

1 Combine chilli sauce, sesame oil, honey, rind, ginger and orange juice and pour over chicken. Cover and refrigerate for at least 1 hour or overnight.

Leave the chicken marinating in the morning and you can have dinner ready in a flash.

2 Thread chicken onto skewers and barbecue or grill, using gentle heat, for no more than 10 minutes, turning once or twice (do not overcook).

3 While chicken is cooking, heat remaining marinade in a small saucepan and boil for 2-3 minutes.

4 Blend cornflour with 1 tablespoon of extra orange juice. Add to sauce and stir until thickened. Serve chicken on steamed rice, top with the sauce and accompany with stir-fried vegetables.

Variation Use 8 chicken drumsticks in place of chicken breast fillets. Place drumsticks and the marinade mixture into a shallow ovenproof dish, cover and bake in a moderate oven for 40 minutes. Blend cornflour with orange juice and use to thicken juices in dish.

Nutritional information/serving: 9.5 g fat, 0 g fibre, 1000 kJ.

Serves 4

500 g skinless chicken thigh fillets, trimmed of fat and cut into 2.5 cm cubes
1 teaspoon chilli sauce
2 teaspoons sesame oil
2 tablespoons honey
1 teaspoon finely grated orange rind

1 teaspoon finely grated ginger
½ cup orange juice
1 teaspoon cornflour
1 tablespoon extra orange juice
Bamboo skewers, soaked in water

FRUITY TURKEY ROAST

1 Place dried fruit medley and ½ cup apricot nectar into a small saucepan, bring to the boil, simmer for 5-6 minutes. Add almonds and cinnamon. Allow to cool.

A new and healthy twist to a roast dinner. Also delicious served cold.

2 Preheat oven to 180°C. While fruit is cooking, cut a pocket in the turkey breast. Stuff cooled fruit and nut filling into pocket. Spread mustard on outside of turkey and place in a greased ovenproof dish. Pour over remaining apricot nectar. Bake in preheated oven for 45-50 minutes, or until brown. Remove turkey to a heated plate, ready for carving.

3 Combine brandy and cornflour. Add to juices in dish in which turkey was cooked and stir until thickened. Slice turkey and serve with sauce.

Microwave In a microsafe dish, cook fruit medley and nectar on high for 3 minutes.

Nutritional information/serving: 5.5-6.5 g fat, 1-1.5 g fibre, 1025-1280 kJ.

Serves 4-5

½ cup dried fruit medley
1 cup apricot nectar
1 tablespoon slivered almonds
½ teaspoon cinnamon

600 g piece of turkey breast
1 tablespoon grainy mustard
2 teaspoons cornflour
2 tablespoons brandy

LAMB STACKS

1 Sprinkle eggplant slices with salt and leave for 15 minutes or until beads of juice appear on surface. Wash well and pat dry.

A simple and delicious meal. You can also use turkey, chicken or thinly sliced lean beef.

2 Place eggplant slices on top of lamb steaks. Spread eggplant with tomato paste, sprinkle with oregano and top with sliced capsicum.

3 Preheat oven to 180°C. Bake stacks in oven for 20 minutes.

4 Top stacks with mozzarella and bake for another 5 minutes, or until cheese melts. Serve at once.

Serve with crusty wholemeal bread and a salad or steamed vegetables.

Nutritional information/serving: 10 g fat, 2.5 g fibre, 1125 kJ.

Serves 4

8 slices of eggplant
Salt
4 lamb steaks, about 600 g
2 tablespoons tomato paste

1 tablespoon chopped oregano or 1 teaspoon dried oregano
1 red capsicum, seeded and sliced
4 slices mozzarella

Handy Hint
To stop pork, steak or chicken curling up while cooking, make some small snips around the edge with kitchen scissors before cooking.

NUTTY PORK STEAKS

1 Combine pine nuts, seeds and thyme and press onto both sides of pork steaks.

This recipe can also be made with chicken fillets.

2 Heat oil in a non-stick pan, gently cook pork for about 10-12 minutes, turning once. Remove and keep warm.

3 Add onion to pan and cook gently for 3-4 minutes, or until softened. Add milk and cream cheese to onion and stir until hot. Do not boil. Serve over pork and sprinkle with thyme.

Serve with potatoes steamed in their jackets and green salad or vegetables.

Nutritional information/serving: 14 g fat, 2 g fibre, 1345 kJ.

Serves 4

1 tablespoon pine nuts

1 tablespoon poppy seeds

2 tablespoons sesame seeds

2 teaspoons dried thyme or 1 tablespoon fresh thyme leaves

4 pork steaks, about 600 g

1 tablespoon olive oil

1 onion, sliced

½ cup low-fat evaporated milk

1 tablespoon light cream cheese

1 tablespoon fresh thyme leaves for garnish

LEMON VEAL

1 Cut lemon in slices and remove pips. Place the lemon, including skin, in blender with garlic, coriander, soy sauce and chilli (all ingredients except veal). Process until smooth.

2 Place veal in a shallow ovenproof dish, pour lemon mixture over, cover and refrigerate for at least 2 hours.

3 Preheat oven to 180°C. Bake for 20-30 minutes.

Serve with noodles tossed with plenty of chopped fresh coriander and steamed vegetables or salad.

The strong tang of the lemon makes this a delightful dish. It is also delicious using chicken drumsticks or skinless chicken thighs instead of veal.

Nutritional information/serving: 1.5 g fat, 1.0 g fibre, 440 kJ.

Serves 4

4 veal T-bone steaks, trimmed of fat	2 tablespoons fresh coriander
1 whole lemon	1 tablespoon salt-reduced soy sauce
1 clove garlic	1 teaspoon chopped chilli

Handy Hint

If you need to flatten pork, veal or chicken fillets, place them between sheets of greaseproof paper and hit them with the flat side of a meat mallet or with a milk bottle.

SESAME LAMB PARCELS

1 Preheat oven to 180°C. Place 1 lamb steak onto the corner of each sheet of filo. Spread lamb steaks with chutney, and top each with sliced mushrooms.

A simple way to serve lamb. The filo pastry seals in the juices and prevents the meat drying out.

2 Fold side edges of pastry over lamb and form into a parcel, sealing edges with a little sesame oil. Place each parcel onto a greased baking tray, brush tops with oil and sprinkle with sesame seeds. Bake in preheated oven for 40-45 minutes. Serve with steamed fresh asparagus or other green vegetable and baked potato slices.

Nutritional information/serving: 10 g fat, 1.5 g fibre, 1155 kJ.

Serves 4

- 4 lean lamb steaks, about 600 g
- 4 sheets filo pastry
- 1 tablespoon fruit chutney
- 100 g mushrooms, sliced
- 2 teaspoons sesame oil, warmed
- 1 tablespoon sesame seeds

OSSO BUCO

1 Preheat oven to 160°C. Heat a heavy-based pan, brown veal on all sides. Place meat into a well-soaked clay pot, or a large ovenproof casserole.

This dish is quick to prepare but needs long, slow cooking. It is ideal to cook one night, refrigerate, and reheat the next day.

2 Add onion and garlic to pan in which veal was cooked and cook over a gentle heat, stirring frequently until onion softens.

3 Add paprika, tomatoes, eggplant, oregano, bay leaves, red wine and 1 teaspoon of lemon rind. Bring to the boil and pour over veal. Cover tightly and cook in preheated oven for 1½ hours.

4 Add mushrooms and cook a further 15 minutes. Just before serving, sprinkle with parsley and lemon rind. Serve with steamed couscous and some brightly coloured steamed vegetables.

Microwave After browning veal, place in a microsafe dish with ingredients as above. Cover and cook on high for 30 minutes then medium for 45 minutes. Add mushrooms and cook on medium for 5 minutes. If the dish is prepared by conventional cooking, it can be reheated on high for 15 minutes before serving.

Nutritional information/serving: 2 g fat, 7.5 g fibre, 965 kJ.

Serves 4

2 veal shanks, cut into chunks	1 teaspoon oregano leaves or 1 tablespoon fresh
1 large onion, sliced	oregano leaves
1 clove garlic, crushed	2 cups red wine
1 tablespoon paprika	1 teaspoon finely grated lemon rind
800 g can tomatoes	300 g whole button mushrooms
1 medium eggplant, peeled and cubed	2 tablespoons chopped parsley for garnish
4 bay leaves	2 teaspoons finely grated lemon rind for garnish

PORK WITH PEACHES

1 Press juniper berries into pork steaks.

2 Heat oil in large frying pan, add pork and cook gently for 7-8 minutes, turning once. Remove pork and keep warm.

3 Add onion to pan and cook over a gentle heat for 3-4 minutes or until onion softens, without browning. Add cinnamon, juice and brandy and bring to the boil.

4 Replace pork in pan and add spring onions and peach slices.

5 Blend cornflour with water, add to pan and stir mixture until it boils and thickens. Serve with steamed new potatoes and vegetables.

Variation If peaches are out of season, use apples or firm pears. Substitute apple juice for the orange juice.

Nutritional information/serving: 6.5 g fat, 1.5 g fibre, 1120 kJ.

Serves 4

1 tablespoon juniper berries, crushed
1 tablespoon macadamia nut oil
4 pork steaks, about 600 g
1 medium onion, finely chopped
½ teaspoon cinnamon
1 cup orange juice

1 tablespoon brandy
½ cup sliced spring onions
2 large peaches, peeled, stoned and sliced
2 teaspoons cornflour
1 tablespoon water

BARBECUED LAMB KEBABS

1 Combine red wine, garlic, rosemary and pepper and pour over lamb. Refrigerate for at least 1 hour.

A great dish for the barbecue or to cook and serve indoors. If using bamboo skewers, soak them for 1-2 hours in cold water to prevent them burning.

2 Remove lamb from marinade, thread cubes onto skewers, alternating with water chestnuts, onion, capsicum and mushrooms.

3 Brush with marinade; barbecue or grill, turning and brushing with marinade mixture frequently. Do not overcook.

Serve with rice tossed with a few toasted pine nuts, and a tossed salad.

Nutritional information/serving: 5 g fat, 3 g fibre, 915 kJ.

Serves 4

½ cup red wine
1 clove garlic, crushed
1 teaspoon dried rosemary or 1 tablespoon fresh rosemary leaves
Freshly-ground black pepper
500 g lean lamb steak, cut into 2.5 cm cubes

200 g can water chestnuts, drained
1 large onion, peeled and cut into 8 wedges
1 capsicum, seeded and cut into 2.5 cm squares
8 button mushrooms
Bamboo skewers, soaked in water

VEAL AND SPINACH ROLLS

1 Sprinkle veal with pepper. Top each steak with 4 spinach leaves.

These rolls can be prepared ahead and reheated when needed.

2 Combine mushrooms, green onions and pine nuts. Add just enough yoghurt to hold mixture together. Place a quarter of the mushroom mixture onto each piece of veal and roll up to form a parcel. Tie with string or secure with skewers.

3 Preheat oven to 180°C. Brown rolls in a non-stick pan, place into a casserole dish just large enough to hold them. Pour wine into dish, cover and bake in preheated oven for 40 minutes. Serve each roll with some of the meat juices.

Good with noodles and a green salad.

Nutritional information/serving: 5 g fat, 4 g fibre, 1020 kJ.

Serves 4

4 thin veal steaks, about 600 g
1 teaspoon coarsely cracked pepper
16 leaves English spinach, stalks removed
1 cup sliced mushrooms

½ cup sliced green onions
1 tablespoon toasted pine nuts
2 tablespoons low-fat yoghurt
¾ cup white wine

CRACKED WHEAT MEAT LOAF

1 Pour water over wheat, leave for 10 minutes until all the water is absorbed.

Serve this meat loaf hot or cold. It can also be made in individual dishes which are ideal with salad and crusty wholemeal bread for a picnic lunch.

2 Combine wheat with beef, carrot, onion, cardamom, mixed spice, pepper and rind. Pack into a greased non-stick loaf tin (12 x 23 cm), patting down firmly. Bake at 180°C for 1 hour. Allow to stand for 5 minutes before turning out.

Serve with steamed vegetables and/or salad.

Microwave Pack mixture into a microsafe loaf dish (12 x 23 cm). Cook on high for 25-30 minutes. Allow to stand 5 minutes before serving.

Nutritional information/serving: 7-10 g fat, 3-4 g fibre, 900-1350 kJ.

Serves 4-6

1 cup cracked wheat
1 cup boiling water
500 g lean minced beef
1 large carrot, grated
1 medium onion, finely chopped

2 teaspoons ground cardamom
½ teaspoon mixed spice
Freshly ground black pepper
1 teaspoon finely grated orange rind

WHISKIED BEEF STEAKS

1 Combine whisky, marmalade and ginger. Pour over steaks and refrigerate for at least 30 minutes.

Quick and easy. As long as you use lean meat, the fat content will be low. If preferred, lean rump steak can be used in place of fillet.

2 Remove meat from marinade and grill under high heat for 3-4 minutes on each side, brushing frequently with marinade.

Serve with baked, whole potatoes topped with low-fat natural yoghurt, grilled eggplant slices and a salad.

Nutritional information/serving: 5.5 g fat, 0 g fibre, 895 kJ.

Serves 4

½ cup whisky
2 tablespoons orange marmalade

1 teaspoon finely chopped ginger
4 small pieces fillet steak, about 500 g

legumes

Dried beans and peas are wonderful sources of fibre, protein, minerals and vitamins. They are also low in fat and contain some valuable anti-cancer agents. As a bonus, they're cheap and easy to store. So why don't we eat them more often? The most common reason for lack of interest in legumes is that most people don't know how to cook them. In fact, they are easy to cook, but with most varieties, you do need to think about cooking them well before you start to feel hungry.

BASIC WAYS TO COOK LEGUMES

1 For legumes which do not need soaking (lentils, split peas, black-eyed beans)
Use 3 cups of water for evey cup of lentils or beans. Bring to the boil and simmer until tender (about 25 minutes for lentils, 40 minutes for split peas or black-eyed beans).
Microwave 15 minutes for lentils, 20 minutes for split peas or black-eyed beans.

2 For all other beans, chickpeas, and other dried peas
Either soak beans overnight, using 3 cups of water for every cup of beans. Drain beans, add another 3 cups of fresh water for every cup of soaked beans, bring to the boil and simmer for 40-80 minutes or until tender.

 To eliminate the overnight soak, place beans and water in saucepan with a tight-fitting lid, using 3 cups of water for every cup beans. Bring to the boil, cook 1-2 minutes, cover and turn off heat. Leave for 1 hour. Drain, add 3 cups of fresh water for every cup of soaked beans, bring to the boil, cover and simmer for 40-80 minutes, until tender.
Microwave Cooking times are approximately half those above.

3 Pressure cooker
After either of the soaking methods above, cook beans until tender, which generally takes about half the normal time. Take care, as beans can clog up the vent on pressure cookers. Also make sure that the volume of beans and water does not fill more than half the pressure cooker.

HOUMMOS

1 Bring chickpeas and water to the boil. Cook for 1 minute, cover tightly, leave to stand for 1 hour. If leaving longer than 1 hour, place saucepan in refrigerator so that peas don't ferment.

This spread can be used with felafel, spread onto pita bread, enjoyed with lavash bread or served with tabbouli salad.

2 Drain peas and cover with fresh water. Bring to the boil, cover and simmer gently for 1 hour. Do not discard cooking liquid.

3 In a food processor or blender, process chickpeas with garlic, tahini and lemon juice, adding enough of the chickpea cooking liquid to make a thick paste.

Nutritional information/serving: 18 g fat, 10 g fibre, 1300 kJ.

Serves 4

1 cup raw chickpeas*
4 cups water
1 clove garlic, crushed

1/3 cup tahini
1/4 cup lemon juice

* If using cooked chickpeas, use 2 1/2 cups. Start from step 3.

FALAFEL

1 Bring chickpeas and water to the boil. Cook for 1 minute, cover tightly, leave to stand for 1 hour. If leaving longer than 1 hour, place saucepan in refrigerator so that peas do not ferment.

These delicious Middle-Eastern patties are good served in pita bread with salad and tahini.

2 Drain chickpeas, cover with fresh water, bring to the boil, cover and simmer gently for 1 hour. Drain.

3 While chickpeas are cooking, steam or microwave potatoes until tender.

4 Place cooked chickpeas, potatoes, onion, garlic, parsley, tahini, yoghurt, lemon juice, cumin and pepper into food processor and blend until well combined.

5 Preheat oven to 180°C. Form mixture into approximately 18 patties. Place on a greased, ovenproof tray and bake in preheated oven for 30 minutes, turning once during cooking.

Serve falafel with a dollop of the sauce, and chopped fresh tomato, cucumber and mint.

For sauce:
1 Combine yoghurt, tahini, lemon juice and rind.

Nutritional information/serving: 5.5 g fat, 3 g fibre, 525 kJ.

Serves 6

1½ cups raw chickpeas*
5 cups water
2 medium-large potatoes, scrubbed
1 medium onion, chopped
1 clove garlic, crushed
½ cup chopped parsley
1 tablespoon tahini
1 tablespoon low-fat yoghurt
2 tablespoons lemon juice
1 teaspoon ground cumin
Freshly ground black pepper

Sauce:
1 cup low-fat yoghurt
1 tablespoon tahini
1 tablespoon lemon juice
1 teaspoon finely grated lemon rind

* If using cooked or canned chickpeas, use 3½ cups.

TUNA WITH BEANS

1   Heat olive oil and gently cook onion and garlic for 3-4 minutes, or until onion softens. Add chilli and cumin and continue cooking for 2-3 minutes longer, stirring constantly.

A quick, healthy dish to prepare using cans from your pantry.

2   Add tomatoes, tomato paste and kidney beans and heat until mixture boils. Carefully stir in tuna and simmer until heated through. Serve over steamed rice, sprinkled with parsley.

Nutritional information/serving: 7.5 g fat, 7 g fibre, 965 kJ.

Serves 4

1 tablespoon olive oil
1 medium onion, chopped finely
1 clove garlic, crushed
1 teaspoon finely chopped chilli
2 teaspoons ground cumin

400 g can tomatoes, no added salt
2 tablespoons tomato paste
400 g can red kidney beans, drained and washed
425 g can tuna in spring water, drained
2 tablespoons chopped parsley

CRUNCHY BEAN DELIGHT

1 Soak beans and chickpeas in a large saucepan of water overnight.

This dish takes little time to prepare initially, but needs long slow cooking. You can also prepare it to the last stage and refrigerate. Add breadcrumbs and bake just before serving.

2 Preheat oven to 160°C. Drain beans and chickpeas and add 6 cups fresh water, onion, celery, tomatoes, tomato paste, wine, sugar, cinnamon stick, bay leaves, rosemary and chilli into a large casserole. Cover and bake in preheated oven for 1 hour. Remove cinnamon stick, bay leaves and rosemary and cook uncovered for a further 45 minutes.

3 Combine breadcrumbs and parsley, sprinkle over beans. Turn oven to 180°C and bake, uncovered, for about 15 minutes, or until crumb topping is crunchy.

Nutritional information/serving: 3 g fat, 15 g fibre, 1140 kJ.

Serves 6

1 cup raw kidney beans	1 tablespoon dark brown sugar
1 cup raw chickpeas	1 piece cinnamon stick
4 cups water	3 bay leaves
1 large onion, chopped	2-3 sprigs fresh rosemary or 1 teaspoon dried
1 stick celery, sliced	1 tablespoon paprika
800 g can tomatoes, no added salt	1 teaspoon chopped chilli
2 tablespoons tomato paste	1 cup fresh wholemeal breadcrumbs
1 cup red wine	½ cup chopped parsley

Handy Hint

Do not add salt to the water when soaking or cooking beans or peas. Salt slows down the absorption of water, so the beans take longer to cook.

SPICY CHICKPEA CASSEROLE

1 Heat oil and gently cook onion, chilli, coriander and cumin for 3-4 minutes, stirring frequently.

This tasty casserole is ideal for vegetarians or those wanting a high-fibre, low-fat meal.

2 Add kumera, cauliflower and stock, bring to the boil, cover and simmer 10 minutes. Add chickpeas, tahini and lemon juice and heat through, stirring well. Serve topped with toasted sesame seeds.

Nutritional information/serving: 11 g fat, 8 g fibre, 925 kJ.

Serves 6

1 tablespoon olive oil

1 onion, peeled and cut into wedges

1 small hot chilli, chopped finely

1 tablespoon dried ground coriander

1 teaspoon ground cumin

2 cups cubed kumera

2 cups cauliflower pieces

1½ cups vegetable stock

2 cups cooked or drained, canned chickpeas

2 tablespoons tahini

2 tablespoons lemon juice

1 tablespoon toasted sesame seeds

BEAN LOAF

1 Put beans into food processor and grind. Add onions, capsicum, carrot, mushrooms, oregano, eggs, cheese and wheatgerm and process until combined.

This loaf is quick and easy. Serve it hot or cold. It's also delicious on sandwiches.

2 Pack into a greased loaf tin which has been lined with baking paper. Bake at 180°C for 35 minutes. Allow to stand for 5 minutes before turning out.

Serve with steamed vegetables or salad.

Microwave Pack mixture into a greased microsafe pan (23 cm x 12 cm). Cook on medium for 15 minutes. Allow to stand 5 minutes before turning out.

Nutritional information/serving: 10 g fat, 11 g fibre, 855 kJ.

Serves 4

2 x 340 g cans soy beans, drained
½ cup sliced spring onions
1 red capsicum, seeded and diced
1 large carrot, grated
1 cup sliced mushrooms

1 teaspoon dried oregano or 2 teaspoons fresh oregano leaves
2 eggs
½ cup grated cheese
½ cup wheatgerm

LENTIL NUTTIES

1 Place lentils, onion and water into a saucepan, bring to the boil, cover and cook over a gentle heat until lentils are tender and mixture is dry, about 20-25 minutes. If lentils are still wet, remove lid, heat gently and stir until the mixture is thick and dry, taking care it does not burn.

> **Popular with children, these crunchy lentil cakes are also good served with salad in pita bread.**

2 Using a food processor, blend cooked lentil mixture, garam masala, almonds, breadcrumbs, parsley, wheatgerm and egg. If you do not have a food processor, chop nuts and parsley and combine all ingredients.

3 Form into 8 patties. Press sunflower seeds into patties.
Preheat oven to 180°C. Bake on a greased tray for 20-30 minutes, turning once.

Serve with Fresh Tomato and Mushroom Sauce (see page 160), steamed vegetables and mashed potatoes.

Microwave Lentils can be cooked in a microsafe dish, covered, on high for 15 minutes. Patties are not suitable to microwave.

Nutritional information/serving: 15 g fat, 10 g fibre, 1445 kJ.

Serves 4

1 cup lentils	2 slices wholemeal bread, made into crumbs
1 medium onion, finely chopped	2 tablespoons parsley
2 cups water	½ cup wheatgerm
1 teaspoon garam masala spice powder	1 egg
½ cup almonds	2 tablespoons sunflower seeds

LENTIL LASAGNE

1 Place lentils, bay leaves and water into a saucepan, bring to the boil, cover and simmer for 20 minutes, or until water has been absorbed. Remove bay leaves.

This is a low-fat lasagne with plenty of dietary fibre. Try them on their own as an entree or separate course.

2 Meanwhile, heat oil and cook onion and garlic over gentle heat until soft but not brown. Add tomatoes, carrot, capsicum, mushrooms and herbs, bring to the boil, cover and simmer, stirring occasionally, for 20 minutes. Stir in lentils.

3 Preheat oven to 180°C. In a greased shallow casserole dish, place ⅓ vegetable mixture. Top with 3 sheets lasagne and ⅓ ricotta cheese. Repeat these layers twice. Sprinkle top with mozzarella and sesame seeds. Bake for 25 minutes.

Microwave Cook lentils with bay leaves and water in microsafe dish on high for 12 minutes. Cook oil with onion and garlic for 2 minutes, add vegetables and herbs, cook on high for 12-15 minutes. Stir in lentils. Assemble lasagne, cook on high for 15 minutes.

Nutritional information/serving: 17 g fat, 8 g fibre, 1655 kJ.

Serves 6

1 cup red lentils	1 cup grated carrot
3 bay leaves	1 capsicum, seeded and sliced
2 cups water	2 cups sliced mushrooms
1 tablespoon olive oil	1 teaspoon mixed Italian herbs
1 large onion, sliced	9 instant lasagne sheets
1 clove garlic, crushed	375 g ricotta cheese
2 cups chopped tomatoes, fresh or canned, no added salt	½ cup grated mozzarella
	¼ cup sesame seeds

MEXICAN DELIGHT

1 Heat oil in a medium saucepan and cook onion for 2-3 minutes, allowing it to brown slightly.

2 Add chilli, paprika and capsicum and stir over a low heat for about 3-4 minutes, or until capsicum has softened. Add tomatoes and beans, bring to the boil and cook for about 2-3 minutes or until thick. Serve with taco shells, shredded lettuce, chopped cucumber, grated cheese and yoghurt.

Microwave Cooking times are the same as those given above.

Nutritional information/serving: 5.5 g fat, 7.5 g fibre, 615 kJ.

Serves 4

1 tablespoon olive oil
1 onion, chopped
1 teaspoon chopped chilli
1 tablespoon paprika

1 red capsicum, seeded and chopped finely
2 large tomatoes, chopped
440 g can red kidney beans

Handy Hint

If beans cause excessive flatulence, discard the soaking water and replace with fresh water to which you have added 1 teaspoon mustard seeds. To reduce flatulence, also make sure you eat the 'skins' which sometimes loosen on beans. These contain minerals which absorb some of the substances which give beans their well-known reputation!

HOME-STYLE BAKED BEANS

1 Soak beans in water overnight.

Canned baked beans are useful and nutritious but if you'd l
to make your own, they taste even better.

2 Drain beans, add 6 cups fresh water, bring to
the boil and simmer 1 hour. Add apple, sugar, mustard, cloves, onion, tomatoes and ham.
Tip mixture into a casserole and bake, covered at 150°C for 1 hour, adding a little more water if
necessary.

Microwave Beans can be cooked in microsafe dish, covered on high for 30 minutes.

Nutritional information/serving: 2.5-4 g fat, 15-22 g fibre, 1090-1635 kJ.

Serves 4-6

2 cups haricot beans or lima beans	Pinch powdered cloves
6 cups water	1 large onion, chopped finely
1 apple, peeled and chopped roughly	410 g can peeled tomatoes
2 tablespoons dark brown sugar	250 g diced lean ham
1 tablespoon dry mustard	

Handy Hint
Some cookbooks suggest adding bi-carbonate of soda when cooking legumes. This is not a good idea as it destroys some
of the vitamins.

COUSCOUS

1 Place couscous into a fine sieve and run under the tap. Tip into a large bowl and leave for about 10 minutes, breaking up any lumps with your fingers.

Couscous is made from semolina and is served in North Africa with chickpeas and vegetables. It tastes much better steamed, preferably twice.

Sprinkle with about ½ cup of water and work gently with your fingers until water has been absorbed.

2 Place couscous into the top of a steamer and steam, uncovered, for 10-15 minutes. Tip into a bowl and stir in butter.

3 Heat oil and cook onion, garlic and spices over a gentle heat for 2-3 minutes.

4 Add eggplant, pumpkin, zucchini, tomatoes, beans, chickpeas and stock. Bring to the boil, cover and simmer for 10 minutes.

5 While vegetables are cooking, replace couscous in steamer and steam for a further 10-15 minutes.

Serve vegetables over couscous, topped with walnuts.

Microwave In microsafe dish, cook oil, onion, garlic and spices on high for 2 minutes. Add remaining ingredients, except walnuts, cook on high for 8-10 minutes. Add walnuts. Serve over couscous.

Nutritional information/serving: 11-17 g fat, 8-12 g fibre, 855-1280 kJ.

Serves 4-6

350 g couscous	1 medium eggplant, cubed
1 tablespoon butter, cut into pieces	3 cups pumpkin chunks
1 tablespoon olive oil	2 large zucchini, sliced thickly
1 large onion, sliced	2 large tomatoes, cut into cubes
1 clove garlic, crushed	250 g green beans, trimmed
2 teaspoons ground cumin	2 cups cooked chickpeas
3 teaspoons ground coriander	1 cup chicken or vegetable stock
1 teaspoon ground turmeric	¼ cup walnuts

CHICKPEAS WITH ENGLISH SPINACH

1 Bring chickpeas and water to the boil. Cook for 1 minute, cover tightly, leave to stand for 1 hour. If leaving longer than 1 hour, place saucepan in refrigerator so that peas do not ferment.

A simple dish for those times when you don't feel like anything exotic.

2 Drain, cover with fresh water, bring to the boil, cover and simmer gently for 45 minutes, or until just tender.

3 Heat oil and cook onion and garlic over gentle heat for 3-4 minutes, or until onion softens.

4 Add chickpeas, lemon rind, tomato and spinach, stir gently and bring to the boil. Simmer for 10 minutes, adding a little water if necessary. Serve with flat bread.

Microwave Cooking times are the same as those given above.

Nutritional information/serving: 9 g fat, 15 g fibre, 1260 kJ.

Serves 4

1½ cups chickpeas*
5 cups water
1 tablespoon olive oil
1 large onion, sliced

1 clove garlic, crushed
1 teaspoon finely grated lemon rind
2 large tomatoes, cut into cubes
1 bunch English spinach, shredded

* If using cooked chickpeas, use about 3 cups. Start from Step 3.

vegetables

Vegetables are amazingly good for you. They supply valuable forms of dietary fibre, many vitamins and minerals, and several thousand other components that may provide protection against many cancers. As a bonus, vegetables have no fat, no salt, and are low in kilojoules.

In spite of their advantages and the great variety available, vegetable consumption is falling. This is largely because they form little part of fast food and take-away meals which now account for one third of the food dollar.

For both taste and nutrition, it's best not to overcook most vegetables. Potatoes are an exception as they need to be well cooked to make them digestible. Some Greek-style vegetables should be cooked until they are quite soft.

ASPARAGUS WITH LEMON SAUCE

1 Bring some water to the boil in a frypan, add asparagus and cook for 3 minutes. Drain and place asparagus into a shallow serving dish which can withstand going under the griller.

Spring is the best time for fresh asparagus, although it is also available in summer and winter.

2 Stir together the ricotta, yoghurt, lemon juice, peel and pepper. Spread over asparagus.

3 Combine crumbs and cheese. Sprinkle over sauce and grill for 2-3 minutes until crumbs are crisp and brown.

Variation Use steamed broccoli, beans, cauliflower or zucchini in place of asparagus.

Nutritional information/serving: 4.5 g fat, 1.5 g fibre, 430 kJ.

Serves 4

1 bunch fresh asparagus	1 teaspoon finely grated lemon peel
1/2 cup ricotta cheese	Freshly ground black pepper
1/2 cup low-fat yoghurt	1/2 cup fresh wholemeal breadcrumbs
1 tablespoon lemon juice	1 tablespoon grated parmesan

Handy Hint
If you can't buy fresh vegetables, frozen ones are the next best thing. Canned vegetables also retain many of their vitamins, especially ones such as tomatoes.

BEETROOT WITH ORANGE SAUCE

1 Cut stems off beetroot, leaving about 2.5 cm. Wash well. Heat orange juice in a saucepan, add beetroot and cinnamon stick. Cover and cook for 30-45 minutes, or until beetroot is tender. Cool a little, slip skins off and trim off stems. Cut into halves or quarters.

Many people have never cooked fresh beetroot. They take time to cook, but the taste is worth the wait. Buy baby beetroot if possible.

2 Remove cinnamon stick from juice. Reheat juice and add beetroot.

3 Blend cornflour and vinegar. Stir into beetroot until mixture thickens.

Nutritional information/serving: 0 g fat, 4 g fibre, 330 kJ.

Serves 4	500 g beetroot	2 teaspoons cornflour
	1 cup orange juice	1 tablespoon red wine vinegar
	1 cinnamon stick	

Handy Hint

There is always some loss of vitamins when vegetables are cooked. Microwaving does the least damage because you don't need to use any water. Steaming is almost as kind. If you must boil your vegetables, use as little water as possible. Keep the water from cooked vegetables in the freezer to use later in stocks or soups.

CRUNCHY BROCCOLI

1 In a non-stick frypan, brown breadcrumbs. Cool.

2 Mix cheese, nuts, breadcrumbs and thyme.

3 Steam broccoli for 6-8 minutes, or until barely tender. Place in shallow ovenproof dish; sprinkle with cheese/crumb mixture and bake at 180°C for 5-10 minutes or until cheese is melted.

A delightful lunch dish or serve as a vegetable with grilled fish or chicken.

Variation Use cauliflower, beans or zucchini in place of broccoli.

Nutritional information/serving: 7.5 g fat, 4.0 g fibre, 470 kJ.

Serves 4

1 slice wholemeal bread, made into crumbs
½ cup grated cheese
1 tablespoon chopped pecan nuts

1 teaspoon dried thyme or 2 teaspoons fresh thyme
300 g broccoli

115

ORANGE-GINGER CARROTS

1 Place carrots, orange juice, rind, ginger and sherry into a medium-size saucepan. Bring to the boil, cover and simmer for 5-6 minutes. Lift carrots from liquid.

Carrots, orange and ginger make a great combination.

2 Boil juice rapidly until reduced by half. Pour over carrots. Serve hot.

Nutritional information/serving: 0 g fat, 4 g fibre, 245 kJ.

Serves 4

500 g carrots, sliced thinly
½ cup orange juice
1 teaspoon finely grated orange rind

1 teaspoon grated fresh ginger
2 tablespoons dry sherry

Handy Hint
Prepare vegetables as close to mealtime as possible. Oxygen in the air destroys some of the vitamins in vegetables.

STIR-FRIED BRUSSELS SPROUTS

1 Heat oils in non-stick frypan and gently cook garlic and onion for 2-3 minutes.

These nutritious little vegetables are delicious served this way

2 Add sprouts and stir-fry for 3-4 minutes, or until barely tender.

Variation Use broccoli, carrots, sliced cauliflower, zucchini, green beans or a mixture of vegetables.

Nutritional information/serving: 5 g fat, 3 g fibre, 290 kJ.

Serves 4

2 teaspoons olive oil

2 teaspoons sesame oil

1 clove garlic, crushed

1 small onion, sliced

300 g Brussels sprouts, trimmed and sliced lengthwise into 4-5 pieces

RED CABBAGE NORMANDY

1   Heat oil and cook onion over a gentle heat for 2-3 minutes without browning. Add cabbage, apple, apple juice, and caraway seeds, cover and cook for 15 minutes. Remove lid, continue cooking until liquid has evaporated. Serve hot or cover and refrigerate until needed. Just before serving, sprinkle sesame seeds on top.

Cabbage is a good source of vitamins and dietary fibre and this dish is delicious served hot or cold. It's an excellent accompaniment to pork or veal dishes.

Variation   Add 2 tablespoons raisins to cabbage. If desired, omit caraway and/or sesame seeds.

Nutritional information/serving: 6 g fat, 5 g fibre, 455 kJ.

Serves 4

1 tablespoon olive oil
1 small onion, diced
½ small red cabbage, shredded
1 apple, peeled, cored and sliced

½ cup apple juice
½ teaspoon caraway seeds
2 teaspoons toasted sesame seeds

BRAISED FENNEL

1 Preheat oven to 180°C. Slice fennel in halves (or quarters if large) and arrange in a small casserole dish.

2 Combine oil, garlic and wine and pour mixture over fennel. Cover and bake for 25 minutes.

Microwave Cook on high for 12-15 minutes.

Nutritional information/serving: 5 g fat, 6 g fibre, 515 kJ.

Serves 2

2 small or 1 large fennel bulb
2 teaspoons olive oil

1 clove garlic, crushed
½ cup white wine

Handy Hint

If your children don't like cooked vegetables, let them eat them raw. They have more vitamins and there is no reason why children should not have plain raw vegetables on their plates at the table.

CAULIFLOWER IN ORANGE SAUCE

1 Steam cauliflower for about 8 minutes, until barely tender (or microwave for 3-4 minutes). Place in a shallow ovenproof dish.

A light and healthy dish for lunch or as an accompaniment to steamed vegetables or salad.

2 Combine yoghurt, orange rind, egg yolk, nutmeg and pepper.

3 Beat egg whites until stiff and gently fold into yoghurt mixture. Spoon egg white mixture over cauliflower and sprinkle with grated cheese. Bake at 180°C for 15 minutes.

Microwave Step 1 only is suitable for microwave.

Variation Use broccoli in place of cauliflower.

Nutritional information/serving: 6.5 g fat, 2.5 fibre, 555 kJ.

Serves 4

500 g cauliflower
200 g low-fat yoghurt
1 teaspoon finely grated orange rind
1 egg, separated

1 extra egg white
Pinch nutmeg
Freshly ground pepper
½ cup grated cheese

STIR-FRIED CELERY AND ALMONDS

1 Toast almonds in a dry wok or frypan, taking care not to burn them. Set aside.

> **Great with steamed rice or tossed over pasta.**

2 Heat oils in frypan or wok, toss celery until hot. Sprinkle with soy sauce and almonds.

Serve as a vegetable or a first course.

Nutritional information/serving: 15 g fat, 3 g fibre, 695 kJ.

Serves 2

2 tablespoons almonds
3 teaspoons olive oil
1 teaspoon sesame oil

2 cups diagonally sliced celery
1 tablespoon light soy sauce

LEEKS VINAIGRETTE

1 Heat chicken stock and thyme, add leeks and simmer for 10-12 minutes, or until tender. Drain, reserving any liquid for soup.

Leeks are one of the most delightful vegetables, especially if you can pull them fresh from your own garden. Try them on their own.

2 Combine olive oil, lemon juice, vinegar and honey. Pour over leeks and serve hot or chilled.

Microwave In a microsafe dish cook chicken stock and thyme on high for 1 minute. Add leeks and cook on high for 8 minutes.

Variation Substitute 8 small whole peeled onions for the leeks.

Nutritional information/serving: 10 g fat, 3.5 g fibre, 565 kJ.

Serves 2

½ cup chicken stock
2-3 sprigs thyme or lemon thyme
2 leeks, cut in halves lengthwise and washed thoroughly

1 tablespoon olive oil
1 tablespoon lemon juice
1 tablespoon wine vinegar
1 teaspoon honey

BAKED KUMERA AND APPLE

1 Preheat oven to 180°C. Place a layer of kumera in a greased, shallow casserole, followed by a layer of apples. Sprinkle apples with cinnamon. Repeat layers until all kumera and apples are used. Pour apple juice over; bake for 25 minutes.

This goes well with pork or veal dishes.

Serve hot, garnished with sprigs of mint.

Microwave Cook on high for 12-15 minutes.

Variation Use regular sweet potato or butternut pumpkin to replace kumera.

Nutritional information/serving: 0 g fat, 6.5 fibre, 650 kJ.

Serves 4   500 g kumera, peeled and sliced thinly   1 teaspoon ground cinnamon
            2 granny smith apples, peeled, cored and sliced   1 cup apple juice
            thinly

SIMPLY DIVINE MUSHROOMS

1 Take a large piece of foil and place mushrooms in the centre. Sprinkle with tarragon and place bay leaves on top. Fold foil into a parcel and bake at 180°C for 10-15 minutes.

Open at the table so the aroma can be fully appreciated.

This is the easiest way of all to cook mushrooms. None of their superb aroma is lost.

Nutritional information/serving: 0 g fat, 3 g fibre, 125 kJ.

Serves 4

500 g mushrooms, buttons or caps
2 bay leaves

½ teaspoon dried tarragon or 2 teaspoons fresh tarragon .

POTATO PANCAKES

1 Using your hands, squeeze as much liquid from potatoes as possible. Place in bowl with onion, eggs, flour and pepper. Stir well and leave mixture to stand 15 minutes.

2 Heat a heavy-based pan and add a film of oil. Place about ¼ cup of potato mixture into small heaps in hot pan and cook until golden brown on both sides.

Serve with lean grilled steak or chicken, or with salad, or with a dollop of stewed apple.

Nutritional information/serving: 3 g fat, 4 g fibre, 905 kJ.

Serves 4

4 large potatoes, peeled and grated
1 small onion, peeled and grated
2 eggs, beaten

⅓ cup plain flour
⅛ teaspoon white pepper

STUFFED MUSHROOMS

1 Remove stems from mushrooms, chop finely. Combine with ricotta, herbs, pepper and lemon rind and use to stuff mushrooms.

These are good as a first course for dinner or as an accompaniment to a main course.

2 Combine crumbs and almonds and sprinkle over mushrooms. Place on foil-lined tray, bake at 180°C for 10 minutes, or until crumbs are golden.

Nutritional information/serving: 5.5 g fat, 1.5 g fibre, 360 kJ.

Serves 4

8 mushroom cups
½ cup ricotta
1 tablespoon mixed fresh herbs such as parsley, lemon thyme, marjoram

Freshly ground black pepper
1 teaspoon finely grated lemon rind
1 slice wholemeal bread, made into crumbs
1 tablespoon flaked almonds

130

AVOCADO-STUFFED POTATOES

1 Scrub potatoes and pierce with a fine skewer in 4-5 places. Place on oven shelf, bake at 180°C for 1 hour, or until tender when pierced with a skewer.

> **One of my favourite dishes. A microwave makes this quick and easy.**

2 Cut a 'lid' from top of potato, carefully remove flesh, leaving a supporting 'wall' inside the skin. Mash potato flesh well, adding yoghurt, avocado, lemon thyme and lemon rind.

3 Pile mixture back into potato shells and replace 'lid'. Bake at 180°C for 15 minutes.

Microwave After scrubbing potatoes and piercing with a fine skewer in 4-5 places, microwave on high for 20 minutes. Pile mixture back into shells and microwave on high for 5 minutes.

Variations
1 Combine potato flesh with ½ cup cottage cheese, ½ cup chopped mushrooms, 2 teaspoons chopped chives and 1 teaspoon French mustard.
2 Combine potato flesh with ½ cup yoghurt, ¼ cup sliced spring onions, and a small can of drained salmon.
3 Combine potato flesh with ½ cup yoghurt, ½ cup sweet corn kernels, 1 teaspoon paprika and 2 tablespoons grated cheese.

Nutritional information/serving: 8 g fat, 4 g fibre, 915 kJ.

Serves 4
4 large potatoes such as desiree or idaho
½ cup natural low-fat yoghurt
1 small or ½ large avocado

1 teaspoon fresh lemon thyme or ½ teaspoon dried thyme, and ½ teaspoon finely grated lemon rind

BAKED POTATO SLICES

1 Cut clove of garlic in half and rub around the inside of a greased, ovenproof dish. Discard garlic. Arrange layers of potatoes and onion, sprinkling each layer with a little pepper.

A delicious way to enjoy potatoes without fat.

2 Pour chicken stock over potatoes, bake uncovered at 180°C for 45 minutes, or until top is brown.

Microwave Cook on high for 18-20 minutes.

Nutritional information/serving: 0.5 g fat, 3 g fibre, 410 kJ.

Serves 4   1 clove garlic   Freshly ground pepper
           4 medium potatoes, sliced thinly   1 cup chicken stock
           1 large onion, peeled and sliced thinly

HEAVEN AND EARTH

1   Cook pumpkin, potato and apple in chicken stock for 15 minutes or until tender. Drain, reserving stock for soup.

A delicious combination. Add a salad and it makes a meal.

2   Preheat oven to 180°C. Mash or purée vegetables, adding ricotta, nutmeg and pepper.

3   Beat egg whites until stiff and gently fold through vegetable mixture. Pile into ovenproof dish.

4   Mix oats, wheatgerm, seeds, cheese and parsley. Sprinkle over vegetable mixture and bake for 20 minutes. Serve hot.

Microwave   In a microsafe dish, cook pumpkin, potato and apple on high for 10 minutes. Drain liquid. The second stage of this dish is not suitable for microwaving.

Variations   Substitute 1 tablespoon sesame or sunflower seed kernels for the poppy seeds.

Nutritional information/serving: 5-7.5 g fat, 4-6.5 g fibre, 775-1165 kJ.

Serves 4-6

400 g pumpkin, peeled and chopped roughly
4 medium potatoes, chopped roughly
2 apples, peeled and cored
1 cup chicken stock
½ cup ricotta cheese
Pinch nutmeg
Freshly ground black pepper

2 egg whites
¼ cup rolled oats
¼ cup wheatgerm
2 teaspoons poppy seeds
2 tablespoons grated cheese
1 tablespoon finely chopped parsley

STIR-FRIED VEGETABLES (without oil)

1   Heat chicken stock in large non-stick frypan or wok and boil until reduced to half its original volume.

Stir-frying with stock is a healthy and delicious way to prepare vegetables.

2   Add onion, garlic and carrots to pan and stir-fry for 2-3 minutes. Add beans, asparagus and snow peas and continue stir-frying for 3-4 minutes. Add mushrooms, and stir-fry until they are hot. Sprinkle vegetables with coriander. Serve hot or cold.

Variation   Omit coriander. Sprinkle vegetables with 1 tablespoon toasted sesame seeds.

Nutritional information/serving: 0.5 g fat, 5 g fibre, 240 kJ.

Serves 4

1 cup chicken stock	1 bunch asparagus spears, cut into 4 cm lengths
1 medium onion, sliced	1 cup snow peas, trimmed
1 clove garlic, crushed	1 cup sliced button mushrooms
1 cup sliced carrot	1 tablespoon chopped coriander
1 cup sliced green beans	

Handy Hint
Avoid using bi-carbonate of soda to make vegetables look brightly coloured. It destroys their vitamins – and tastes horrible.

SPAGHETTI SQUASH SPECIAL

1 Steam the whole squash for about 25 minutes. Allow to cool for 5-10 minutes.

This amazing vegetable is just like crunchy spaghetti. Use it in place of spaghetti, or as a vegetable.

2 Meanwhile, heat oil, add garlic and pine nuts and cook for about 2 minutes, or until pine nuts are brown.

3 Add basil, pepper and fennel to pan and toss until heated.

4 Cut squash in halves lengthwise, remove seeds. Using a fork, pull strands of the squash from the sides. When all the 'spaghetti' has been removed, toss gently with fennel mixture until hot.

Microwave Pierce squash with a skewer in several places and microwave on high for 12 minutes. Proceed with Step 2.

Nutritional information/serving: 6 g fat, 11 g fibre, 485 kJ.

Serves 4

1 spaghetti squash, approximately 1 kg
2 teaspoons olive oil
1 clove garlic
1 tablespoon pine nuts

1 cup fresh basil leaves, torn
Freshly ground black pepper
1 cup thinly sliced fennel

PESTO-STYLE TOMATOES

1 Toast pine nuts in a dry frypan until golden brown.
Set aside.

Make this in summer when fresh basil is available.

2 Combine basil, parsley, breadcrumbs, oil and pine nuts.

3 Cut each tomato in half and scoop out a little of the flesh. Pile basil mixture onto tomato halves, pressing firmly. Bake at 180°C for 10-15 minutes or until topping is crunchy.

Nutritional information/serving: 8 g fat, 4 g fibre, 480 kJ.

Serves 4

¼ cup pine nuts
1 cup fresh basil leaves
¼ cup chopped parsley

½ cup fresh wholemeal breadcrumbs
2 teaspoons olive oil
4 medium tomatoes

salads

When salads are an interesting, flavoursome, colourful collection of healthy ingredients they stimulate the appetite. This chapter includes some salads that are traditionally served as accompaniments to other foods, but made with healthy dressings. There are also some that you can whip up for a quick, complete meal. Or try a delicious warm salad, especially good for lunch on a crisp autumn day.

WARM CRUNCHY CHICKEN SALAD

1 Poach chicken breasts in barely simmering water with peppercorns and ginger for 12 minutes. Turn off heat and leave chicken in water for 5 minutes. Drain chicken, pull off skin. (Freeze chicken stock for other recipes.)

> A warm salad is perfect on a hot summer night, or for winter or autumn lunches. This one is a complete meal.

2 Meanwhile, toast nuts in a dry frypan, shaking constantly over gentle heat until golden brown. Set aside.

3 Steam broccoli for 3-4 minutes. Immediately plunge into cold water. Drain well.

4 Combine ingredients for dressing in a jar, shake well.

5 Arrange warm chicken fillets on individual plates. Surround with broccoli, capsicum and onion. Top with nuts. Pour ¼ dressing over each serving. Garnish with a sprig of lemon thyme or thyme.

Microwave In a microsafe dish cook broccoli on high for 2 minutes.

Nutritional information/serving: 20 g fat, 4 g fibre, 1420 kJ.

Serves 4

4 chicken breasts, about 500 g
6 peppercorns
Small piece of fresh ginger
¼ cup walnut halves
1 tablespoon pine nuts
2 cups broccoli pieces
1 red capsicum, seeded and sliced
1 small red onion, sliced

Dressing:
1 tablespoon olive oil
1 tablespoon walnut oil
2 tablespoons wine vinegar
1 teaspoon honey
2 teaspoons fresh lemon thyme or thyme leaves or
¼ teaspoon dried thyme

Handy Hint
Try different salad greens. Look out for radicchio, mignonette, oak, coral or cos lettuce, the slightly bitter arugula (great in a salad to serve with pasta), curly endive, witlof (also known as Belgian endive) and sour lemon sorrel.

WARM TURKEY SALAD WITH MANGO SAUCE

1 Heat oil in a large frypan and cook turkey or chicken for about 10 minutes, turning until lightly browned.

Serve with new potatoes steamed in their jackets and lightly tossed with chopped chives and parsley. Add some crusty bread to make an ideal light meal.

2 Meanwhile, combine mango, chutney, lime juice, mustard and port in blender, process until just combined (there should still be some texture of the mango remaining).

3 Arrange lettuce and radicchio on plate. Slice cooked turkey or chicken fillets, arrange on top of lettuce. Pour sauce over and serve at once.

Nutritional information/serving: 9.5 g fat, 2.5 g fibre, 1150 kJ.

Serves 4	500 g turkey breast fillets (or use chicken breast fillets)	1 tablespoon lime or lemon juice
	1 tablespoon olive oil	2 teaspoons Dijon mustard
	1 large mango, peeled and sliced	¼ cup port
	2 tablespoons mango chutney	Mignonette lettuce
		Radicchio leaves

RAW FISH AND MUSHROOM SALAD

1 Place fish into a glass bowl. Cover with lemon or lime juice, refrigerate for at least 3 hours, by which time the fish flesh will have softened and become opaque.

A delightful dish on a hot, summer's day. The lemon or lime juice makes the flesh of the raw fish wonderfully tender.

2 Drain fish and arrange with mushrooms and coriander sprigs in a salad bowl.

3 Combine garlic, olive oil and lemon juice. Pour over salad. Refrigerate for 10-15 minutes, then remove garlic pieces. Toss gently and sprinkle with dill.

Variation The fish can also be poached in a little fish stock or white wine for 10 minutes. Cool and proceed with Step 2.

Nutritional information/serving: 11 g fat, 1.5 g fibre, 855 kJ.

Serves 4

400 g gemfish or other white fish fillets, sliced into strips
1 cup lemon or lime juice
2 cups sliced button mushrooms
½ cup fresh coriander sprigs or parsley
1 tablespoon fresh dill

Dressing:
1 clove garlic, cut in halves
2 tablespoons olive oil
2 tablespoons lemon or lime juice

SMOKED SALMON AND PASTA SALAD

1 Cook pasta according to directions on packet until al dente. Drain well.

An easy dish for friends or family that can be prepared quickly. Using smoked salmon pieces will reduce the cost.

2 Toast pine nuts in a dry frypan, shaking over a gentle heat until golden brown. Set aside to cool.

3 Steam snow peas for 2-3 minutes (they should be crisp). Immediately rinse under cold water, drain well. Combine with pasta, salmon, capsicum, rind and peppercorns.

4 Combine dressing ingredients together, pour over salad. Just before serving, sprinkle pine nuts over the top.

Variation Replace smoked salmon with canned red salmon or tuna.

Nutritional information/serving: 13 g fat, 6.5 g fibre, 1660 kJ.

Serves 4	250 g pasta spirals or shells	Dressing:
	1 tablespoon pine nuts	2 tablespoons orange juice
	1 cup snow peas, topped and tailed	1 tablespoon white wine vinegar
	100 g smoked salmon, sliced	2 tablespoons extra virgin olive oil
	1 green capsicum, seeded and sliced	1 tablespoon chopped fresh mint
	2 teaspoons finely grated orange rind	Freshly ground black pepper
	2 teaspoons drained pink peppercorns	½ cup low-fat yoghurt

AVOCADO TUNA SALAD

1 Steam broccoli and snow peas for 2-3 minutes (they should still be crisp). Immediately run cold water over vegetables and drain well.

A complete, easy summer meal.

2 Combine broccoli, peas, tuna, avocado, celery and capsicum. Toss gently together and arrange on lettuce leaves.

3 Mix yoghurt with lemon rind, juice and thyme. Drizzle over salad and top with pine nuts.

Nutritional information/serving: 16 g fat, 6 g fibre, 1200 kJ.

Serves 4

1 cup broccoli pieces
1 cup snow peas
425 g can tuna in spring water, drained
1 ripe avocado, peeled, stoned and cut into chunks
1 cup sliced celery
1 red capsicum, seeded and sliced
1 coral leaf lettuce, washed
1 tablespoon toasted pine nuts

Dressing:
½ cup natural yoghurt
1 teaspoon finely grated lemon rind
2 tablespoons lemon juice
1 tablespoon chopped lemon thyme, thyme or
¼ teaspoon dried thyme

Handy Hint

Avocado will go brown if left exposed to the air for more than about half an hour. Brushing with lemon juice helps a bit, but it's best to always add avocado to any salad just before serving.

PITA BREAD SALAD

1 Combine yoghurt, pepper, parsley, celery, carrot, salmon, eggs and tomato and toss gently together.

An easy lunch, especially popular with children as the ingredients do not readily fall out of the pita bread.

2 Cut a slice from the top of each pita bread and spoon ¼ filling into each. Top with sprouts.

Nutritional information/serving: 8 g fat, 3.5 g fibre, 1235 kJ.

Serves 4

½ cup natural yoghurt
¼ teaspoon lemon pepper
1 tablespoon chopped parsley
½ cup sliced celery
½ cup grated carrot

220 g can salmon, drained and flaked
2 hard-boiled eggs, shelled and chopped
1 large tomato, diced
4 pita breads
½ punnet snow pea sprouts

ROASTED CAPSICUM SALAD

1 If you have a gas stove, place capsicums on a long fork and hold close to the gas flame until skin blackens and blisters. If you have an electric stove, place capsicums under a hot griller, turning frequently until black and blistered. Place capsicums into a paper bag, seal and leave for 5-10 minutes.

2 When capsicums are cool enough to handle, remove skins and seeds, catching any juices. Cut capsicum flesh into long strips.

3 Add garlic, olive oil, pepper, vinegar and capers to capsicum and any remaining juices. Leave to stand for 20-30 minutes for flavours to mingle.

In early autumn when sweet red capsicums abound, try this wonderful salad. It is superb with a small piece of lightly grilled fillet steak and steamed new potatoes.

Nutritional information/serving: 10 g fat, 2.5 g fibre, 560 kJ.

Serves 4	3 large red capsicums	2 tablespoons olive oil
	1 tablespoon capers, drained	Freshly ground black pepper
	1 clove garlic, crushed	1 tablespoon balsamic vinegar

CELERIAC WITH CREAMY DRESSING

1 Peel celeriac, cut into thin strips. Toss with lemon juice to prevent browning.

Celeriac is a root vegetable with a delicate celery-like flavour, usually available during autumn and early winter. Make this salad ahead and leave to stand before serving for the best flavour.

2 Combine vinegar, lemon juice, mustard, tarragon, yoghurt and ricotta and blend until smooth. Pour over celeriac, toss gently and cover with plastic wrap. Refrigerate for ½–1 hour. Just before serving, decorate salad with cherry tomatoes.

Nutritional information/serving: 1.5 g fat, 7 g fibre, 340 kJ.

Serves 4

1 celeriac, about 500 g
¼ cup lemon juice
1 punnet of cherry tomatoes

Dressing:
1 tablespoon tarragon vinegar
1 tablespoon lemon juice
2 tablespoons Dijon mustard
2 teaspoons fresh chopped tarragon or ½ teaspoon dried tarragon
½ cup low-fat yoghurt
1 tablespoon smooth ricotta cheese

NUTTY BEAN SALAD

1 Steam beans for 3-4 minutes (they should be crisp). Strain and run cold water over them. Drain well and chill.

2 Toast almonds in a dry frypan, shaking over gentle heat until golden brown. Set aside.

3 Combine garlic, macadamia oil, vinegar, lemon juice and pepper in blender. Add half the almonds and switch blender on and off a few times so that nuts are chopped but not ground too finely.

4 When ready to serve, place beans, watercress and mushrooms into salad bowl. Pour dressing over salad, toss gently to combine and sprinkle remaining almonds on top.

Nutritional information/serving: 17 g fat, 7.5 g fibre, 855 kJ.

Serves 4

500 g green beans, topped and tailed
⅓ cup slivered almonds
2 cups button mushrooms, sliced
Small bunch watercress, washed and with coarse
stalks removed

Dressing:

1 clove garlic, crushed
2 tablespoons macadamia nut oil
1 tablespoon wine vinegar
1 tablespoon lemon juice
Freshly ground pepper

COLESLAW WITH HERBED HONEY DRESSING

1 Blend orange juice, orange rind, honey, macadamia nut oil and thyme in blender or food processor.

This is a coleslaw with a fine dressing. Serve it with fish or grilled chicken.

2 Combine cabbage, apple, celery and dressing. Refrigerate for 30 minutes. Just before serving, add pecans.

Nutritional information/serving: 11 g fat, 4 g fibre, 620 kJ.

Serves 4

Dressing:
2 tablespoons orange juice
1 teaspoon finely grated orange rind
2 teaspoons honey
2 tablespoons macadamia nut, or extra virgin olive oil
1 tablespoon fresh thyme leaves or ½ teaspoon dried thyme

3 cups shredded cabbage
1 cup finely sliced apple
1 cup finely sliced celery
1 tablespoon pecan nuts

CRACKED WHEAT SALAD

1 Place wheat and apricots into a bowl and add boiling water. Cover and stand for at least 30 minutes, or until all water has been absorbed.

Cracked wheat is popular in Middle-Eastern countries and is highly nutritious.

2 Add ginger, lemon juice and toasted coconut.

Nutritional information/serving: 1.5 g fat, 4 g fibre, 600 kJ.

Serves 4
¾ cup (120 g) cracked wheat
½ cup dried apricots, chopped
1 cup boiling water

1 teaspoon finely chopped fresh ginger
2 tablespoons lemon juice
1 tablespoon toasted coconut

WALDORF SALAD

1 Place nuts in a dry frypan and shake over a gentle heat until lightly browned. Cool.

2 Toss celery, apples, grapes and nuts together.

3 Combine yoghurt, lemon juice and pepper and mix into salad.

Originally created for the opening of the Waldorf Hotel in New York, this salad usually has a rich, fat-laden dressing. This lighter version is much kinder to your arteries.

Nutritional information/serving: 11 g fat, 4.5 g fibre, 880 kJ.

Serves 4

½ cup walnuts or pecans
2 cups diced celery
2 red apples, cored and diced
1 cup sultana grapes

Dressing:
1 cup natural low-fat yoghurt
2 tablespoons lemon juice
Freshly ground black pepper

POTATO SALAD

1 Steam potatoes in their jackets for about 15 minutes until just cooked. While potatoes are hot, cut in halves, place into a bowl and pour white wine over them. Cover and leave until cool.

Potato salad is a great source of complex carbohydrate. The usual dressings provide a lot of fat but this one is low on fat but high on flavour.

2 Combine yoghurt, mustard and lemon juice. Add to potatoes, with chives, mint and parsley. Toss well. Serve sprinkled with paprika.

Microwave Cook potatoes on high for 8-10 minutes.

Nutritional information/serving: 2 g fat, 2 g fibre, 615 kJ.

Serves 4

500 g small new potatoes
½ cup white wine
¾ cup natural yoghurt
1 teaspoon Dijon mustard

1 tablespoon lemon juice
1 tablespoon each chopped chives, mint and parsley
Paprika for garnish

154

TABOULEH

1 Place cracked wheat into a bowl and pour boiling water over, cover tightly, leave until cool. (Wheat will have absorbed water and should be quite dry.)

A great source of complex carbohydrates and one of the few ways to eat enough parsley to take advantage of its superb nutritional value. Try it with pita bread or with cubes of lean lamb grilled on skewers.

2 Add green onions, parsley, mint and tomatoes.

3 Combine lemon juice, olive oil, garlic and pepper. Use a fork to fluff up the cracked wheat and add dressing. Toss well.

Nutritional information/serving: 10 g fat, 9 g fibre, 1010 kJ.

Serves 4

1 cup cracked wheat
2 cups boiling water
½ cup finely chopped green onions
1½ cups finely chopped parsley
½ cup finely chopped mint
4 medium tomatoes, cut into small dice

Dressing:

2 tablespoons lemon juice
2 tablespoons extra virgin olive oil
1 clove garlic, finely chopped
Plenty of freshly ground black pepper

Handy Hint

Use a good, extra virgin olive oil in a dressing and you'll find you can use less oil for more flavour. Some salads are also good with flavoured vinegars, used with or even instead of any oil.

sauces and dressings

Sauces make many foods more appetising, but most traditional sauces are rich and fatty. Try some of the recipes in this chapter for healthier ways to add flavour to foods.

WHISKIED APRICOT SAUCE

1 Boil water, cinnamon and cloves for 10 minutes. Remove cinnamon and cloves.

A spicy sauce which is ideal to serve with pork, chicken or turkey.

2 Add apricots, green onions and ginger to water and simmer for 10 minutes, stirring frequently.

Nutritional information/serving: 0 g fat, 3 g fibre, 330 kJ.

Serves 4

¾ cup water
Piece cinnamon stick
6-8 cloves
1 cup chopped apricots

¾ cup finely sliced green onions
1 teaspoon finely grated fresh ginger
1 tablespoon whisky

157

SPICED BLUEBERRY SAUCE

1 Place cinnamon stick, cloves, sugar, orange juice and vinegar into a small saucepan, bring to the boil and simmer gently for 5 minutes.

2 Add blueberries, cook a further 2-3 minutes.

Serve warm or cold with chicken, duck, turkey, pork, veal or venison.

Nutritional information/serving: 0 g fat, 1 g fibre, 215 kJ.

Serves 4
1 cinnamon stick	½ cup orange juice
2 cloves	1 tablespoon raspberry vinegar
1 tablespoon dark brown sugar	1 punnet of blueberries

TANGY LIME SAUCE

1 Place juice, vinegar and thyme into a small saucepan and boil uncovered for 3 minutes. Remove thyme and add mustard.

A delicious sauce to serve with fish, barbecued prawns or with scallops.

2 Pour beaten egg into lime mixture, stirring constantly until sauce thickens.

Nutritional information/serving: 1.5 g fat, 0 g fibre, 110 kJ.

Serves 4   ¼ cup lime or lemon juice   2 teaspoons Dijon mustard
             ¼ cup white wine vinegar   1 egg, beaten
             Few sprigs thyme

FRESH TOMATO AND MUSHROOM SAUCE

1 Heat olive oil and cook onion and garlic over a gentle heat without browning for 4-5 minutes.

The simple taste of a dish of steaming pasta served with a home-made sauce is hard to beat.

2 Add tomatoes, wine and oregano and simmer, uncovered, for 15 minutes. Add mushrooms and cook for a further 5-8 minutes.

Serve over hot cooked pasta.

Nutritional information/serving: 5 g fat, 4.5 g fibre, 475 kJ.

Serves 4

1 tablespoon olive oil
1 onion, finely slice
1 clove garlic, crushed
1 kg ripe tomatoes, chopped and peeled

½ cup red wine
1 teaspoon dried oregano leaves
2 cups sliced mushrooms

PEANUT SAUCE

1 In a small saucepan, heat oil and cook onion and garlic for 3-4 minutes over a gentle heat, without browning.

This sauce contains some fat but if you serve it with lots of vegetables, which have almost no fat, the whole meal will still be low in fat.

2 Add tamarind, lime juice, peanuts, chilli, coconut milk and water. Simmer, uncovered, for 15-20 minutes, stirring occasionally.

Nutritional information/serving: 23 g fat, 2.5 g fibre, 1030 kJ.

Serves 4

1 tablespoon olive oil
1 medium onion, chopped finely
1 clove garlic, crushed
1 tablespoon tamarind pulp*
2 tablespoons lime or lemon juice

¾ cup chopped peanuts
1 teaspoon chopped chilli
½ cup canned coconut milk
1 cup water

* available from Asian food stores

PESTO SAUCE

1 Place basil, garlic, oil and lemon juice into a food processor or blender and process until fine. Add pine nuts and parmesan and blend until just combined. Serve tossed into hot pasta or over steamed new potatoes or sliced tomatoes, green beans or asparagus.

Fresh basil is one of the delights of summer. Pasta with pesto is delicious. Or use it to make vegetables more interesting. I also love it spread on wholegrain toast and topped with sliced, ripe tomatoes.

Nutritional information/serving: 20 g fat, 2.5 g fibre, 840 kJ.

Serves 4

2 cups fresh basil leaves

1 clove garlic

¼ cup olive oil

2 tablespoons lemon juice

2 tablespoons toasted pine nuts

2 tablespoons grated parmesan

HERBED DRESSING

1 Combine all ingredients, mixing with a fork until well blended.

Too much dressing will drown a salad. Use just enough to giv[e]
flavour.

Nutritional information/serving: 9.5 g fat, 0 g fibre, 355 kJ.

Serves 4 1 tablespoon red wine vinegar ½ teaspoon mustard
2 tablespoons extra virgin olive oil Freshly ground black pepper

164

TAHINI DRESSING

1 Combine all ingredients. Refrigerate until required.

This thick dressing can be used on top of salad vegetables piled into pita bread.

Nutritional information/1/4 cup: 4 g fat, 1 g fibre, 405 kJ.

Makes 1 cup

1 cup low-fat natural yoghurt

1 tablespoon tahini paste

1 tablespoon lemon juice

1 tablespoon fresh chopped coriander

165

BUTTERSCOTCH CUSTARD SAUCE

1 Stir brown sugar and golden syrup together in a small saucepan over a low heat until blended. Add 1 cup milk and heat until hot but not boiling.

> A true butterscotch sauce contains butter, cream and sugar. This recipe has no fat. Unfortunately we cannot dispense with the sugar or there would be no butterscotch flavour at all.

2 Blend remaining milk, egg and cornflour. Add to hot mixture, stirring constantly until thick and smooth. Add vanilla.

Serve with stewed or canned pears or peaches (no added sugar) or over baked apples.

Nutritional information/serving: 1.5 g fat, 0 g fibre, 400 kJ.

Serves 4	1 tablespoon dark brown sugar	1 egg
	1 tablespoon golden syrup	1 tablespoon cornflour
	1½ cups skim milk	½ teaspoon vanilla essence

166

YOGHURT DRESSING

1   Mix all ingredients. Refrigerate until required.

Try this tangy dressing as a low-fat alternative to mayonnaise. Great with hot potatoes, potato salad or coleslaw.

Nutritional information/1/4 cup: 0 g fat, 0 g fibre, 150 kJ.

Makes 1 cup

1 cup low-fat natural yoghurt
2 tablespoons lemon juice
1 teaspoon finely grated lemon rind

Freshly ground black pepper
Pinch sweet paprika

CREAMY PEACH SAUCE

1 Place all ingredients in blender, process until smooth and thick. Refrigerate until required.

Add this sauce to fresh pawpaw or fruit salad for a delightful brunch, lunch or dessert dish.

Nutritional information/serving: 7 g fat, 1 g fibre, 550 kJ.

Serves 4
1 cup canned peaches (no added sugar)
1 cup ricotta

1 tablespoon orange juice
1 tablespoon Cointreau

RASPBERRY SAUCE

1 Combine water and honey, stir over gentle heat until smooth. Boil 2-3 minutes without stirring. Cool a little.

Delicious served over chilled slices of fresh mango or peach. In winter, try it over hot baked pears or apples.

2 Place one punnet of raspberries into blender, add brandy and honey mixture and blend until smooth. Strain and add remaining raspberries.

Nutritional information/serving: 0.5 g fat, 5.5 g fibre, 375 kJ.

Serves 4

½ cup water

2 tablespoons honey

1 tablespoon brandy

2 punnets of raspberries

170

desserts

It's hard to beat fresh fruit for dessert. With the amazing variety of high quality fruits available in Australia and New Zealand, delicious desserts take minimum effort.

For those who want something more, the recipes in this chapter are fairly healthy. All are low in fat, some do contain sugar. Sugar supplies kilojoules and no essential nutrients at all, so the quantities of both sugar and honey have been kept to a minimum. They have not been omitted altogether in all recipes because some dishes made without sugar simply taste as if the cook has forgotten the sugar.

FROZEN BANANA WHIP

1 Place bananas in freezer wrap and freeze until solid. Remove from freezer, chop roughly into bowl of a food processor and beat until thick and creamy.

There can't be a dessert that's more simple than this. It is so healthy that it can be eaten at any time. Serve it in crisp cones for children.

At first you think nothing is going to happen, but the mixture will eventually go thick and creamy and double in bulk. Best eaten at once, but can be frozen for a day or two.

Nutritional information/serving: 0 g fat, 3 g fibre, 500 kJ.

Serves 6   6 bananas, peeled

CITRUS-BERRY FRUIT SALAD

1 Slice grapefruit and oranges into a bowl. Add berries.

2 Combine yoghurt, lemon juice, sugar and cinnamon. Serve on top of fruit and sprinkle with pecans.

Nutritional information/serving: 2-4.5 g fat, 3-6 g fibre, 545-1040 kJ.

Serves 2-4

2 grapefruit, peeled and pith removed
3 oranges, peeled and pith removed
1 cup blueberries
1 cup low-fat natural yoghurt

1 tablespoon lemon juice
2 teaspoons brown sugar
Pinch cinnamon
1 tablespoon toasted pecan nuts

Handy Hint
Oranges and lemons will juice much more easily if they are warm. Pop the fruit into the microwave on high for 20-30 seconds before squeezing.

BLUEBERRY YOGHURT DELIGHT

1 Gently fold egg whites into yoghurt. Layer yoghurt, apple sauce and blueberries into glasses and refrigerate for 30 minutes before serving.

Another simple dessert which can double as a brunch dish.

Nutritional information/serving: 0.5 g fat, 2.5 g fibre, 780 kJ.

Serves 2

2 egg whites, beaten stiffly
1½ cups low-fat natural yoghurt

½ cup apple sauce
1 punnet blueberries

Handy Hint

In summer, serve frozen fruits. Frozen sultana grapes, chunks of peeled melon, peach or apricot halves, bananas and orange quarters are popular alternatives to sweets. Remember to peel bananas first. Wrap in freezer wrap and place on bottom of freezer so that they don't go brown.

MANGO SORBET

1   Place mango flesh into blender and purée until smooth.

A great dessert for a hot day.

2   Beat egg whites until stiff, gradually adding sugar.

3   Fold egg white mixture into mango purée and freeze in an ice-cream churn or freeze in a cake tin until firm. Move from freezer to refrigerator to soften for ½ hour before serving.

Variation   Substitute the flesh of 5 oranges for the mangoes.

Nutritional information/serving: 0 g fat, 1 g fibre, 460 kJ.

Serves 6   3 mangoes, skin and stones removed   ½ cup castor sugar
            2 egg whites

BAKED RICOTTA CHEESECAKE

1 Place all ingredients for crust in food processor, blend until crumbly. Press into a greased 20 cm spring-form tin.

Not quite the same as a rich cheesecake but a delicious light dessert with very little fat and only a fraction of the kilojoules.

2 Beat egg whites until firm. Add sugar, beating until sugar is dissolved.

3 Combine ricotta, yoghurt, lemon juice and rind. Fold in egg white mixture and pour into spring-form tin. Bake in a cool oven (120°C) for 40 minutes. Turn off oven and leave cheesecake in oven until cool. Refrigerate until ready to serve. Just before serving, top with fresh fruits.

Variation If desired, omit crust.

Nutritional information/serving: 10 g fat, 4.5 g fibre, 1100 kJ.

Serves 6

Filling:
3 egg whites
3 tablespoons sugar
2 cups (500 g) ricotta
1 cup low-fat natural yoghurt
3 tablespoons lemon juice
2 teaspoons finely grated lemon rind

Topping:
Fresh fruit such as passionfruit, strawberries or blueberries

Crust:
¼ cup rolled oats
⅔ cup dates, pitted
2 tablespoons lemon juice

CREAMY RHUBARB

1 Cut rhubarb into 3-4 cm lengths. Heat apple juice and sugar in a large saucepan and add rhubarb. Cook over a low heat for about 10 minutes, or until rhubarb is tender. Cool.

Rhubarb is technically a vegetable but has usually been used as a fruit. It contains dietary fibre and very few kilojoules.

2 Purée rhubarb until smooth, adding red currant jelly, ricotta and yoghurt. Pour into individual glass dishes and chill for at least 1 hour.

Microwave Rhubarb and apple can be cooked on high for 5 minutes.

Nutritional information/serving: 7.5 g fat, 5.5 g fibre, 875 kJ.

Serves 4

1 bunch rhubarb, washed and with leaves removed
½ cup apple juice
2 tablespoons sugar (optional)

1 tablespoon red currant jelly
1 cup ricotta
1 cup non-fat natural yoghurt

178

SUMMER PUDDING

1   Line a pudding basin with bread slices, fitting the slices well together so that there are no gaps.

One of the most delightful of all desserts. Use whatever berries are available – mulberries, strawberries, blueberries, blackberries, or a mixture.

2   Gently heat sugar and lemon juice, stirring until sugar dissolves. Add berries and stir gently for 2 minutes, or until some of the juices begin to run from the berries.

3   Place berries into bread-lined basin. Top with more bread, pushing bread in slightly to soak up juices. Cover with a small plate or saucer and place a weight on the plate. Refrigerate for at least 12 hours. Unmold and serve with a pouring custard sauce.

Nutritional information/serving: 1.5 g fat, 5 g fibre, 715 kJ.

Serves 6   8-10 slices of bread with crusts removed   Juice of 1 lemon
             2 tablespoons sugar   5 cups berries

BAKED APPLES

1 Make a shallow cut around centre of apples so that they won't burst when cooking. Stuff centre of apples with raisins and nuts.

An easy but delicious winter dessert.

2 Preheat oven to 180°C. Place apples into an ovenproof dish just large enough to hold them. Pour apple juice over the top and bake for about 20 minutes. Serve hot with creamy peach sauce.

Microwave Cook on high for 5-8 minutes, depending on number of apples being cooked. A single apple will take about 2 minutes.

Nutritional information/serving: 2 g fat, 3.5 fibre, 740 kJ.

For each person:

1 apple, cored

1 tablespoon raisins

2 pecan nuts

½ cup apple juice

Handy Hint

To prevent baked apples bursting, make a thin sharp cut around the middle of the apple skin.

APRICOT PEARS

1 Soak apricots in orange juice for 1 hour, or overnight.

A great dessert to serve hot or cold.

2 Bring apricot mixture to the boil, cover and simmer for 20-30 minutes. Cool a little, then purée until smooth. Add sherry.

3 Poach pears in extra orange juice for 10 minutes until just tender. Serve with apricot sauce. If desired, sprinkle with toasted flaked almonds.

Nutritional information/serving: 0.5 g fat, 7.5 g fibre, 810 kJ.

Serves 4

1 cup dried apricots
1½ cups orange juice
1 tablespoon sherry

4 large pears, peeled and cored
4 tablespoons orange juice

APPLE CRUMBLE

1 Preheat oven to 180°C. Place apples in base of an ovenproof dish (or use 6 individual dishes).

2 Mix remaining ingredients until well combined (a food processor makes it easy) and sprinkle over apples. Bake for about 25 minutes, or until top is crunchy.

Serve with Creamy Peach Sauce (page 169).

This is a crunchy crumble, packed with fibre. It is ideal to make in individual dishes as it tends to live up to its name when being served from a larger dish! My children always called this 'Mummy's Apple Muddle' as I tend to vary the quantity of each ingredient every time I make it – but it's always delicious.

Variations
1 Use rolled barley flakes in place of oats.
2 Use pecans, walnuts, pine nuts or almonds in place of hazelnuts.

Nutritional information/serving: 15-22 g fat, 6-8.5 g fibre, 1175-1760 kJ.

Serves 4-6

800 g can pie pack apples
1 teaspoon cinnamon
1 cup rolled oats
¼ cup flaked coconut
¼ cup brown sugar

¼ cup wheatgerm
¼ cup unprocessed bran
¼ cup pepitas or sunflower seeds
¼ cup roasted hazelnuts
2 tablespoons butter

FLAMING BANANAS

1 Place bananas in a shallow ovenproof dish.

A spectacular dessert which you can prepare in just a few minutes.

2 Preheat oven to 180°C. Combine sugar, orange peel, juice, and cinnamon and pour over bananas. Bake for 10 minutes.

3 Warm rum or brandy. Remove bananas from oven, light rum or brandy and pour over bananas. Serve at once.

Microwave Cook bananas on medium for 4 minutes. Heat rum or brandy on high for 15-20 seconds.

Variations
1 Substitute 4-6 fresh sliced peaches for bananas.
2 Use 4 peeled, halved and cored pears in place of bananas.
3 Omit brown sugar.

Nutritional information/serving: 0 g fat, 3 g fibre, 725 kJ.

Serves 4

4 bananas, peeled and sliced lengthwise
1 tablespoon brown sugar
1 teaspoon finely sliced orange peel (no pith)

¼ cup orange juice
Pinch cinnamon
¼ cup rum or brandy

Handy Hint
If you brush a little lemon juice over apple, pear or banana, they will not go brown so quickly when exposed to air.

184

PEACH SOUFFLE

1 Purée peaches with ginger.

2 Preheat oven to 170°C. Beat egg whites until
stiff, add castor sugar and continue beating until peaks form. Gently fold egg whites into peach purée.
Spoon into individual souffle dishes and bake in preheated oven for 15-20 minutes, or until well-risen.
Serve at once.

A light-as-air dessert which is quick and easy to make.

Variation Use 1 cup apple purée in place of peach.

Nutritional information/serving: 2 g fat, 3.5 g fibre, 740 kJ.

Serves 6 1 cup cooked dried peaches (no added sugar), drained   3 egg whites
½ teaspoon finely chopped preserved ginger (optional)   2 tablespoons castor sugar

muffins, loaves and sweet treats

This is a difficult chapter for any healthy cookbook. Most cakes just don't taste the same without sugar and fat and it makes sense for healthy eaters to keep cakes for special occasions and satisfy the desire for sweet foods with fresh, naturally sweet fruits.

There are some recipes, however, which taste quite acceptable with very little or even no sugar. Some are included in this chapter. Oat and oat bran muffins are now popular and healthy additions to the diet. Wholemeal fruit loaves are also useful foods for those who need concentrated sources of energy, or for those who are physically active and need more kilojoules.

APPLE-SUNFLOWER OAT BRAN MUFFINS

1 Preheat oven to 190°C. Place oat bran, baking powder, cinnamon, and sugar or honey in a large bowl or food processor and mix well. Add apple, eggs, apple juice and milk and process until just combined. Do not overmix or muffins will be tough.

A great way to add oat bran to your diet. Delicious served warm for a weekend brunch.

2 Stir in seeds and spoon mixture into greased or paper-lined muffin pans, filling each three-quarters full. Bake for 20 minutes, or until lightly browned and firm to the touch.

Nutritional information/serving: 4 g fat, 4.5 g fibre, 510 kJ.

Makes
12 large
muffins

2 cups oat bran
3 teaspoons baking powder
2 teaspoons cinnamon
1/4 cup brown sugar or honey
1 large apple, peeled, cored and grated

2 eggs, beaten
3/4 cup apple juice
1/2 cup evaporated skim milk
1/4 cup sunflower seeds

BANANA OAT MUFFINS

1 Preheat oven to 190°C. In food processor or mixer, place flour, oats, baking powder, sugar, rind, cinnamon, cottage cheese, eggs, buttermilk, bananas and raisins. Process until just mixed.

The banana gives a delightful flavour and moistness to these muffins.

2 Spoon mixture into greased or paper-lined muffin pans, filling each three-quarters full. Bake for 20 minutes, or until lightly browned and firm to the touch.

Nutritional information/serving: 3.5 g fat, 3.5 g fibre, 805 kJ.

Makes 12 large muffins

1½ cups wholemeal self-raising flour
1 cup rolled oats
½ teaspoon baking powder
½ cup raw sugar
1 teaspoon finely grated lemon rind
1 teaspoon cinnamon

½ cup cottage cheese
2 eggs
1 cup buttermilk*
2 medium bananas, mashed
½ cup raisins

* or use evaporated skim milk

188

OAT BRAN MUFFINS

1 Preheat oven to 190°C. Place oat bran, baking powder, sugar or honey and sultanas into a large bowl or food processor. Add eggs, milk, oil and vanilla; mix until just combined (do not overmix or muffins will be tough). Stir in nuts.

A basic oat bran muffin which you can eat warm or freeze until required.

2 Spoon into greased or paper-lined muffin pans, filling each three-quarters full. Bake for 20 minutes, or until lightly browned and firm to the touch.

Nutritional information/serving: 9.5 g fat, 5 g fibre, 800 kJ.

Makes 12 large muffins

2½ cups oat bran
2½ teaspoons baking powder
¼ cup brown sugar or honey
½ cup sultanas
2 eggs, beaten

1 cup skim milk
¼ cup light olive, canola or macadamia nut oil
½ teaspoon vanilla essence
¼ cup chopped walnuts

Handy Hint
Oat bran gives a drier product than rolled oats. If using oat bran in place of rolled oats, add a little more of the liquid ingredients.

BERRY OAT MUFFINS

1 Preheat oven to 190°C. In large mixing bowl or food processor, place flour, oats, baking powder, cinnamon and orange peel. Stir ingredients together. Process until just combined.

Try these for afternoon tea.

2 Warm honey slightly by standing over a saucepan of boiling water, add to dry ingredients with oil, buttermilk, eggs and berries. Mix just enough to moisten all ingredients – the mixture should be lumpy. Stir in nuts.

3 Place in greased or paper-lined muffin pans, filling each three-quarters full. Bake for 25 minutes, or until lightly browned and firm to the touch.

Microwave In a microsafe dish, heat honey on high for 20 seconds.

Nutritional information/serving: 11 g fat, 4.5 g fibre, 1080 kJ.

Makes 12 large muffins

2 cups wholemeal self-raising flour
1¼ cups rolled oats
1 teaspoon baking powder
2 teaspoons cinnamon
Grated peel of 1 orange
½ cup honey

¼ cup light olive, canola or macadamia nut oil
¾ cup buttermilk or evaporated milk
2 eggs, beaten
1 cup blueberries or chopped stawberries
½ cup pecan nuts

APPLE SLICE

1 Preheat oven to 180°C. Process bread into crumbs. Add oats, cinnamon, lemon juice and egg, press into a greased tin (20 cm x 30 cm). Bake for 10 minutes.

This slice is best made several hours before you need it. It cuts even better the next day.

2 Meanwhile, combine remaining ingredients, except egg whites. Mix well, gently fold in egg whites. Pour over cooked base mixture and bake for another 40 minutes. Cool in tray, cut into squares to serve.

Nutritional information/piece: 2 g fat, 1.5 g fibre, 350 kJ.

Makes 24 pieces

2 slices wholemeal bread
1 cup rolled oats
1 teaspoon cinnamon
1 tablespoon lemon juice
1 egg or 2 egg whites
1 cup ricotta or cottage cheese
½ cup yoghurt

1 cup sultanas
400 g canned pie pack apple
½ cup wholemeal flour
2 teaspoons finely grated lemon rind
1 teaspoon cinnamon
2 egg whites, stiffly beaten

BRAN AND SUNFLOWER LOAF

1 Place bran cereals, milk, vanilla, peel, raisins and golden syrup into a bowl, cover and leave for at least 2 hours.

High in dietary fibre and a delightful snack for active people.

2 Preheat oven to 180°C. Add flour and ¼ cup sunflower seeds to bran mixture. Spoon into a greased, paper-lined loaf tin, top with remaining seeds. Bake for 45 minutes. Turn out, cool and slice to serve.

Nutritional information/slice: 2.5 g fat, 4 g fibre, 390 kJ.

Makes 16 slices

1 cup processed bran cereal
½ cup unprocessed bran
1½ cups skim milk
1 teaspoon vanilla
½ cup mixed peel

½ cup raisins
1 tablespoon golden syrup
1 cup wholemeal self-raising flour
½ cup sunflower seeds

Handy Hint
Wholemeal flour has more than twice as much dietary fibre, more than twice the level of minerals and about three times as much of most vitamins as white. When using wholemeal plain flour in cakes, use about 10 per cent more baking powder to give a light product.

FRUITY CARROT LOAF

1 Place dates, water, sugar and bicarbonate of soda in a saucepan, bring to the boil, simmer 5 minutes. Cool.

A simple loaf which slices beautifully the next day. A great snack for bushwalkers.

2 Preheat oven to 180°C. Add carrot, walnuts and flour, stirring well. Spoon into a greased, paper-lined loaf tin and bake for 40 minutes. Turn out, cool thoroughly before slicing.

Nutritional information/slice: 2.5 g fat, 4 g fibre, 390 kJ.

Makes 16 slices

1 cup dates	1 cup grated carrot
1 cup water	½ cup walnuts
½ cup brown sugar	1½ cups wholemeal self-raising flour
1 teaspoon bicarbonate of soda	

Handy Hint

To grease a cake tin, heat a small amount of oil and paint over surface of tin with a pastry brush.

HEARTY HEALTH BREAD

1   Preheat oven to 180°C. Mix together kibbled wheat, wheatgerm, bicarbonate of soda and salt. Add honey and buttermilk or yoghurt and stir well to combine.

This is a heavy bread which is delicious cut into very thin slices and spread with low-fat cream cheese or used for sandwiches.

2   Spoon mixture into a greased, lined loaf tin. Bake for about 1¼ hours, or until top feels firm when 'knocked' with knuckle. Turn out and leave for several hours until thoroughly cold before cutting into very thin slices to serve.

Nutritional information/slice: 5 g fat, 3 g fibre, 595 kJ.

Makes 12
slices

1½ cups kibbled wheat
¾ cup wheatgerm
1 teaspoon bicarbonate of soda
Pinch salt

1 tablespoon honey
2 cups buttermilk or low-fat yoghurt
¾ cup sunflower seeds

SCOTTISH OAT CRACKERS

1 Place oats, sugar, bi-carbonate of soda and cinnamon into food processor and process until oats are fine.

No rolling dough for these simple crackers. Delicious spread with low-fat cream cheese.

2 Add butter and milk and mix to make a firm dough. Pat into a square sausage shape, firming well. Wrap in plastic wrap, refrigerate for 1-2 hours.

3 Preheat oven to 175°C. Cut oat mixture into thin slices and place on greased baking trays and bake for 20 minutes. Allow to cool. Store in an airtight container.

Nutritional information/cracker: 1.5 g fat, 0.5 g fibre, 145 kJ.

Makes approximately 40 crackers

3 cups rolled oats
1 tablespoon sugar
½ teaspoon bicarbonate of soda
¼ teaspoon cinnamon
30 g butter or margarine
¼ cup milk

DRIED FRUIT BALLS

1 Combine dried fruit medley, raisins and dates. Pour boiling water over fruits and leave for 15 minutes.

When you want something to 'nibble' with a cup of tea, these little morsels are naturally sweet and scrumptious.

2 Add skim milk powder, nuts and half the coconut and mix thoroughly. Using clean hands, form into 2 cm balls, roll in remaining coconut. Refrigerate, covered, for a few hours before serving.

Variation Press mixture into a slab tin which has been sprinkled with coconut. Press remaining coconut on top.

Nutritional information/ball: 2 g fat, 1 g fibre, 250 kJ.

Makes
about 35

1 cup dried fruit medley (apples, apricots, sultanas)
¾ cup raisins
½ cup dates, chopped
½ cup boiling water

1 cup skim milk powder
½ cup chopped nuts
½ cup desiccated coconut

index

Apple
  see also Heaven and earth,
    Waldorf salad
  baked 180
  baked, with kumera 126
  crumble 182
  slice 192
  sunflower oat bran muffins
    187
Apricot
  pears 181
  sauce, whiskied 157
Asparagus with lemon sauce
  113
Avocado
  and tuna salad 144
  soup, chilled 16
  stuffed potatoes 131
Baked apples 180
Baked beans, home-style 108
Baked kumera and apple 126
Baked potato slices 132
Baked ricotta cheesecake 177
Baked whole bream 53
Bananas
  flaming 184
  frozen whip 172
  oat muffins 188
  smoothie 13
Barbecued lamb kebabs 91
Barbecued ocean trout 54
Barbecued octopus 61
Barbecued tipsy chicken 69

Barley
  and mushroom casserole 43
  buns 44
  stuffed capsicums 48
Basil and ham-stuffed chicken
  thighs 75
Beans
  see also Home-style baked
    beans, Mexican delight
  crunchy delight 100
  loaf 103
  nutty salad 148
  with tuna 99
Beef steaks, whiskied 95
Beetroot
  soup 21
  with orange sauce 114
Berry
  see also Blueberries, Summer
    pudding
  and citrus fruit salad 173
  oat muffins 190
Blueberry
  spiced, sauce 158
  yoghurt delight 174
Braised fennel 120
Bran and sunflower loaf 193
Bread see Hearty health bread
Bream, baked whole 53
Broccoli, crunchy 115
Brussels sprouts, stir-fried 118
Burgers, salmon 67
Butterscotch custard sauce 166

Cabbage see Red cabbage
  Normandy
Cajun chicken 78
Capsicum
  barley-stuffed 48
  roasted, in salad 146
Carrots
  fruity loaf 194
  orange-ginger 116
Cauliflower in orange sauce 122
Celeriac with creamy dressing
  147
Celery and almonds, stir-fried
  123
Cheesecake, baked ricotta 177
Chicken
  and ricotta roulades 79
  barbecued tipsy 69
  basil and ham-stuffed thighs
    75
  Cajun 78
  spicy barbecued 72
  spicy peanut drumsticks 70
  steamed 74
  Thai 76
  warm crunchy salad 139
  with camembert 71
  with honey chilli sauce 80
Chickpeas
  see also Crunchy bean delight,
    Falafel, Farmhouse soup,
    Hommmos
  spicy casserole 102
  with English spinach 111

Citrus-berry fruit salad   173
Coleslaw with herbed honey
        dressing   150
Couscous   110
Cracked wheat
        see also Tabouleh
        loaf   40
        meat loaf   94
        salad   151
Creamy peach sauce   169
Creamy rhubarb   178
Crepes, oat bran   6
Crunchy bean delight   100
Crunchy broccoli   115
Custard sauce, butterscotch   166
Dried fruit balls   198
Falafel   98
Farmhouse soup   26
Fennel, braised   120
Fettuccine carbonara   32
Fish
        see also Seafood
        Mediterranean casserole   57
        raw, and mushroom salad   141
        roulades   58
        stir-fried with mushrooms   56
        with rosemary   50
Flaming bananas   184
French toast   10
Fresh tomato and mushroom sauce
        160
Fresh tomato soup   20
Frozen banana whip   172
Fruit salad
        citrus-berry   173
        Winter   2
Fruity carrot loaf   194
Fruity turkey roast   82
Ginger see Orange-ginger carrots
Ham see Basil and ham-stuffed
        chicken thighs
Hearty health bread   196
Heaven and earth   133
Herbed dressing   164
Home-style baked beans   108
Hoummos   97
Kumera and apple, baked 126

Lamb
        barbecued kebabs   91
        parcels with sesame   87
        stacks   83
Lasagne
        see also Tuna pastitsio
        lentil   106
        vegetarian   29
Leeks vinaigrette   124
Lemon veal   86
Lentils
        lasagne   106
        nutties   104
        soup   25
Lime, tangy sauce   159
Mango sorbet   176
Marmalade, in the microwave   12
Meat loaf, with cracked wheat   94
Mediterranean fish casserole   57
Mexican delight   107
Muesli, Swiss   5
Muesli, toasted   4
Muffins
        apple-sunflower oat bran   187
        banana oat   188
        berry oat   190
Mushrooms
        and barley casserole   43
        and fresh tomato sauce   160
        and raw fish salad   141
        and scallops on skewers   60
        simply divine   127
        stuffed   130
        with stir-fried fish   56
Nutty bean salad   148
Nutty pork steaks   84
Oat bran
        crepes   6
        muffins   189
        muffins, apple-sunflower   187
Oatcakes   8
Oat crackers, Scottish   197
Oats
        see also Oatcakes, Scottish oat
            crackers
        and banana muffins   188
        berry muffins   190

Oaty vegetable omelette   9
Ocean trout see Barbecued ocean
        trout
Octopus, barbecued   61
Omelette, oaty vegetable   9
Orange-ginger carrots   116
Osso buco   88
Pancakes, potato   128
Pasta
        and smoked salmon salad   142
        fettuccine carbonara   32
        prawn and orange   30
        spaghetti with chicken livers
            33
        with pesto   35
        with salmon   28
        with spring vegetables   38
Peaches
        creamy sauce   169
        souffle   185
        with pork   90
Peanut
        see also Spicy peanut drumsticks
        sauce   162
Pears
        and apricots   181
        and plum soup, chilled   17
Pesto sauce   163
Pesto-style tomatoes   137
Pita bread salad   145
Plum, and pear soup, chilled   17
Pork
        nutty steaks   84
        with peaches   90
Potato
        see also Heaven and earth
        and leek soup   15
        baked slices   132
        pancakes   128
        salad   154
        stuffed with avocado   131
        stuffed with tuna   65
Poultry see Chicken, Turkey
Prawns
        with orange and pasta   30
        spicy   62

Pumpkin
  see also Heaven and earth
  soup   18
Raspberry sauce   170
Raw fish and mushroom salad
  141
Red cabbage Normandy   119
Rhubarb, creamy   178
Rice
  fragrant   36
  pie crust   46
  vegetarian Spanish   39
  stuffed tomatoes   42
  tuna pie   47
Ricotta
  and chicken roulades   79
  baked cheesecake   177
Rosemary fish   50
Roasted capsicum salad   146
Roulades
  chicken and ricotta   79
  fish   58
Salmon
  burgers   67
  smoked, salad with pasta   142
Scallops and mushrooms on
  skewers   60
Scottish oat crackers   197
Seafood
  avocado tuna salad   144
  baked whole bream   53
  barbecued ocean trout   54
  barbecued octopus   61
  fish roulades   58
  Mediterranean fish casserole
    57
  pasta with salmon   28
  prawn and orange pasta   30
  raw fish and mushroom salad
    141
  rosemary fish   50
  salmon burgers   67

scallops and mushrooms on
  skewers   60
sesame herbed tuna steaks   52
smoked salmon and pasta
  salad   142
soup   22
spicy prawns   62
stir-fried fish with mushrooms
  56
tuna pastitsio   64
tuna-stuffed potatoes   65
tuna with beans   99
Sesame
  herbed tuna steaks   52
  lamb parcels   87
Silverbeet, bacon and garlic soup
  24
Simply divine mushrooms   127
Smoked salmon and pasta salad
  142
Smoothie, banana   13
Sorbet, mango   176
Souffle, peach   185
Spaghetti squash special   136
Spaghetti with chicken livers   33
Spiced blueberry sauce   158
Spicy barbecued chicken   72
Spicy chickpea casserole   102
Spicy peanut drumsticks   70
Spicy prawns   62
Spinach
  see also Chickpeas with
    English spinach
  and veal rolls   92
Steamed chicken   74
Stir-fries
  brussels sprouts   118
  celery and almonds   123
  fish with mushrooms   56
  vegetables (without oil)   134
Stuffed mushrooms   130
Summer pudding   179

Swiss muesli   5
Tabouleh   155
Tahini dressing   165
Tangy lime sauce   159
Thai chicken   76
Toasted muesli   4
Tomatoes
  and mushroom sauce   160
  pesto-style   137
  rice-stuffed   42
  fresh, soup   20
Trout see Barbecued ocean trout
Tuna
  and avocado salad   144
  pastitsio   64
  rice pie   47
  sesame herbed steaks   52
  stuffed potatoes   65
  with beans   99
Turkey
  fruity roast   82
  warm salad with mango sauce
    140
Veal
  and spinach rolls   92
  osso buco   88
  with lemon   86
Vegetables
  see also Oaty vegetable
    omelette, Pasta with Spring
    vegetables
  stir-fried (without oil)   134
Vegetarian lasagne   29
Vegetarian Spanish rice   39
Waldorf salad   152
Warm crunchy chicken salad   139
Warm turkey salad with mango
  sauce   140
Whiskied apricot sauce   157
Whiskied beef steaks   95
Winter fruit salad   2
Yoghurt dressing   168